SIMPLE & ENTICING RECIPES

PASCOE PUBLISHING, INC.

ROCKLIN, CALIFORNIA

Copyright © 2005 Cuisinart

Cover and Interior Design by Knockout Books

Published in the United States of America by

Pascoe Publishing, Inc.
Rocklin, California
www.pascoepublishing.com

ISBN: 1-929862-44-X

05   06   07   10   9   8   7   6   5   4   3   2

Printed in China

CREDITS AND ACKNOWLEDGEMENTS:

Mary Rodgers, *Editorial Direction* — Teresa Corvino, *Project Manager*

Lee Wooding, *Test Kitchen Manager* — Melissa Abbazia, *Art Direction*

Mark Hennessey, *Photographer* — Roberta Rall, *Food Stylist*

Special thanks to: Barry Haber and Jill Orent

TABLE OF CONTENTS

Chapter Six:

ENCHANTING DESSERTS —◦ 117

INTRODUCTION

Descriptive words are sprinkled throughout this and all other cookbooks in order to define the wonder and joy of preparing and eating food. It's difficult to put the sensory delight of a warm chocolate sauce into words and it is even more challenging to convey the feeling that comes from a particularly delightful meal, well-prepared and lovingly served. But, words do help tell us what to expect from a particular food, recipe or menu plan, whether we are experienced chefs or new to the kitchen. Inside the pages of this book, you will find wonderfully descriptive words and recipe titles designed to create the expectation of a delicious outcome.

When you first look through the recipes in this book, you'll see that each of these recipes has been created with you, your friends and family in mind. Appetizer recipes such as *Baked Brie with Sautéed Apples and Brown Sugar, Croustades with Artichoke and Prosciutto Filling,* and *Endive with Shrimp Filling,* act as merely a gentle introduction to the inviting meal to come. Or, when you are dining very casually with friends, a selection of three of these appetizers might be considered the entire meal.

With busy schedules that often demand fast meal preparation, you'll find that the soups, salads and sandwiches in this book save the day in particularly delicious ways. Consider *Mixed Field Greens with Fennel, Apples & Lemon Mustard Dressing, Provençal White Bean Soup,* and *Grilled Fresh Mozzarella, Tomato & Basil Panini Sandwiches.* When you have time to enjoy the warm glow of baking, recipes like *Parmesan Polenta Rolls, Roasted Shallot and Rosemary Popovers,* and *Focaccia Romana* offer distinctive flavors that make your baked goods worthy of any casual or elegant table. *Souffléd Chevre & Green Onion Potatoes, Oven Roasted New Potatoes & Asparagus,* and *Vegetable Grigliata* offered in Chapter Four remind us that "side dishes" are to the entrée what appropriate accessories are to high-fashion couture. Select side dishes from the recipes in this chapter that enhance the entrée you've chosen.

The main focus of an inviting dinner, the entrée, acts as the star performer and recipes such as *Chicken with Tarragon Mushroom Sauce, Pan Roasted Shrimp and Scallops with Creamy Spinach Feta Sauce over Farfalle* and *Beef Fillets with Green Peppercorn Sauce* are just a few examples of delightful entrées that await your enjoyment. Any evening can be a special one with a bit of attention to fresh herbs, choice cuts of meat, poultry or seafood and a creative splash of seasonings.

A dessert is truly only defined as a "grand finale" when it is worthy of the spotlight. But, just as an appetizer or side dish, it needs to complement the entrée and add only the sweetness and indulgence that the meal preceding it allows. Following the mellow warmth of a successfully served dinner, the invitation of a grand finale dessert can only be eagerly accepted. Desserts like *French Apple Pie, Fresh Pear Sorbet,* and *Chocolate Panini* remind us again of the promise of words used to describe such delights—sweet, warm, fresh, tart—each one a rich reward.

This cookbook is full of delicious and inviting recipes and your anticipation of these delights will be rewarded. The ingredients suggested in each of these recipes are the best and the freshest. By using only the finest, most flavorful foods and spices, your finished dishes offer a combination of the best of flavors. Fresh spinach tastes sweeter, fresh mushrooms have a crisp, earthy flavor, a vanilla bean produces a rich, full-bodied flavor, all of which enhance the final taste of your food. This is a vital step in food preparation. You will find fresh herbs, creamy fresh cheeses, tender cuts of meat and tangy citrus fruits used in unique combinations produce something special for your family and guests.

Each recipe in this cookbook has been rated to give you an idea of the cooking ability involved—beginner, moderate, advanced—but don't let ratings keep you from making any of the wonderfully delicious recipes we have included. Every recipe can be made by the beginner in each of us…it may just take us a bit longer to master the fine details. The end result will be just as delectable!

Our awareness of healthy cooking and eating is important. We have provided nutritional information for each recipe so that you are able to make choices in your meal planning and preparation. If the amount of sodium, carbohydrates, cholesterol, or fiber is important to your particular type of diet, or if you simply like to be aware of what you consume, these nutritional analyses are for you. You will find that the recipes have been developed with a healthy lifestyle in mind.

The delicious appetizers, soups, salads, breads, side dishes, entrées and desserts in this cookbook are made using Cuisinart® appliances to chop, dice, blend, sauté, bake and roast your way to perfection. We hope you enjoy the true essence of superior flavors and the sense of accomplishment that these recipes bring to you and your home.

THE RATING WHISKS:

= beginner/very easy

= easy/moderate

= moderate

= difficult/challenging

Chapter One:

LIVELY APPETIZERS

Appetizers are an invitation. The invitation simply reads, "Please prepare your palate for the exquisite food to follow." As such, appetizers can be easily prepared and thoughtfully presented, but you only need to serve small portions to your family and friends. A serving of *Endive with Shrimp Filling* can be two small leaves. A few pieces of *Crostini with Fig & Plum Tapenade* create just the right amount of interest in the meal to come. A small handful of crudités, stone-ground wheat crackers or blue-corn tortilla chips are ample when partnered with *Simple Salsa Cruda, Mushroom Walnut Paté* or *Eggplant Caviar.*

When you consider the work involved in preparing a meal, you may be tempted to grab a box of crackers and a carton of onion dip at the grocery store instead of preparing an appetizer. But, you will be pleasantly surprised by how easy these appetizers are to make and what a distinctive introduction to your meal they become. Served with a crisp wine or sparkling drink, these appetizers will remind you to take a deep breath, savor a moment to relax and look forward to the meal ahead.

MUSHROOM WALNUT PATÉ

Serve as an hors d'oeuvre with sliced French bread, pita wedges, bagel chips or crackers.

MAKES ABOUT 2 1/2 CUPS

4 ounces	walnut pieces, lightly toasted
1 (2 oz.)	shallot, peeled, cut in 1-inch pieces
2 cloves	garlic, peeled
12 ounces	mushrooms, cleaned
3 tablespoons	unsalted butter
1 teaspoon	herbes de Provence
2 tablespoons	dry sherry or brandy
10 ounces	lowfat cream cheese, cut in 1-inch chunks
1/2 teaspoon	Tabasco® or other hot pepper sauce

Place the walnuts in a Cuisinart® Food Processor fitted with the metal chopping blade and pulse 15 to 20 times to finely chop the walnuts. Remove the walnuts and reserve. With the machine running, drop the shallot and garlic down the feed tube and process for 10 to 15 seconds to finely chop. Remove the vegetables and reserve. Finely chop the mushrooms in 2 or 3 batches, pulsing 15 to 20 times for each batch.

Over medium heat, melt the butter in a Cuisinart® 3 1/2-quart Saucepan. Add the chopped garlic, shallots, mushrooms, and herbes de Provence and cook until the vegetables are tender and the mushrooms have given up all of their juices, about 15 to 20 minutes. Increase the heat to medium high and stir in the sherry or brandy. Cook until the liquid is evaporated. Spoon the vegetables and mushrooms into a bowl and cool.

Using the Cuisinart® Food Processor, soften the cream cheese using the pulse. Add the cooled mushroom mixture and process to combine. Add the chopped walnuts and combine. Transfer the paté to a crock or serving bowl and chill for at least 3 hours. The paté may be made 2 days ahead.

Nutritional information per serving (2 tablespoons):
Calories 91 (71% from fat) carb. 3g pro. 3g fat 8g sat. fat 3g chol. 10mg sod. 85mg calc. 28mg fiber 0g

GREEN & YELLOW TOMATO SALSA ❦

Great with the traditional tortilla chips, or use as a sauce for grilled meats and seafood.

MAKES ABOUT 5 CUPS

1 clove	garlic, peeled
1-2	jalapeño peppers, cored, seeded and quartered
1 small	onion (red or white, about 2 ounces), peeled, cut in 1/2-inch pieces
1/2 cup	medium fresh cilantro leaves, packed
1 pound	firm green tomatoes, cored and cut in 1-inch pieces
1 pound	firm, ripe yellow tomatoes, cored and cut in 1-inch pieces
1 teaspoon	kosher salt
1 teaspoon	ground cumin
1/2 teaspoon	ground coriander
2 tablespoons	fresh lime juice

With the Cuisinart® Food Processor fitted with the metal chopping blade running, drop the garlic and jalapeño peppers through the small feed tube and process to chop, about 10 seconds. Scrape the work bowl. Add the onion and cilantro leaves to the work bowl and pulse to chop about 8 to 10 times. Scrape the work bowl again. Add the tomatoes and pulse 10 to 15 times and scrape the work bowl. Add the salt, cumin, coriander and lime juice and pulse 5 times to combine. Transfer to a medium bowl and refrigerate for at least 30 minutes to allow the flavors to blend. Salsa is at its best when served the day it is made. It will, however, keep for a day or two under refrigeration. Stir if the salsa separates during refrigeration.

Note: Green tomatoes are readily available during the summer and early autumn. You may also use heirloom green tomatoes, which are available in well-stocked grocery stores that carry specialty vegetables. Yellow tomatoes can also be found in most well-stocked grocery stores.

Nutritional information per serving:
Calories 13 (10% from fat) carb. 3g pro. 1g fat 0g sat. fat 0g chol. 0mg sod. 73mg calc. 7mg fiber 1g

APPLE CRANBERRY SALSA

Salsa, the Mexican word for "sauce" can be either fresh or cooked. Fruit based salsas are a refreshing change to the popular tomato based salsas, and are excellent when served with grilled chicken, pork or seafood.

MAKES ABOUT 5 CUPS

2/3 cup	dried cranberries
1/2 cup	cilantro leaves, washed and dried (moderately packed, may use half cilantro and half parsley)
1 small (4 oz.)	red onion, peeled, cut into 1-inch pieces
2 to 3	jalapeño peppers, cored and seeded, cut in 1-inch pieces
1	lime, peeled (remove all white pith), halved
2 to 3 tablespoons	rice or fruit flavored vinegar
1 to 2 teaspoons	honey
1 1/2 pounds	slightly tart apples, washed, cored, cut into 1-inch pieces
1 teaspoon	kosher salt

Place the dried cranberries in a Cuisinart® Food Processor° fitted with the metal chopping blade and pulse 15 to 20 times to chop. Place the cranberries in a large bowl and reserve. Place the cilantro in the work bowl and pulse 10 times. Stir the chopped cilantro into the cranberries. Place the onions in the work bowl and pulse 10 to 15 times. Add jalapeño peppers to the work bowl and pulse 5 to 10 times. Add the chopped onions and peppers to the cranberries and cilantro and stir.

With the food processor running, drop the lime halves through the feed tube and process until completely juiced, about 10 seconds. With the machine running, add the 2 tablespoons of rice vinegar and 1 teaspoon of honey and process to combine about 10 seconds. Add the apple pieces to the work bowl and pulse 15 to 20 times. Add the chopped apple mixture to the large bowl along with salt. Toss gently to combine. Add more vinegar and honey as needed. Cover and refrigerate for 30 minutes to allow flavors to develop.

° *If you have a small capacity food processor, cut the recipe in half or process the apples in 2 batches.*

Nutritional information (per 1/2 cup serving):
Calories 74 (1% from fat)   carb. 19g   pro. 1g   fat 0g   sat. fat 0g   chol. 0mg   sod. 138g   calc. 6mg   fiber 3g

BAKED BRIE WITH SAUTÉED APPLES AND BROWN SUGAR

This delicious fruit and cheese combination makes an enticing hors d'oeuvre.

MAKES 12 SERVINGS

1 sheet	frozen puff pastry (see note)
1 large	egg
1 tablespoon	water
1 large	Granny Smith apple, peeled, cored, cut in half vertically
2 tablespoons	unsalted butter
1/4 cup	firmly packed light brown sugar
1 (8 oz.)	Brie cheese round, sliced in half horizontally

Thaw the puff pastry sheet at room temperature for 30 minutes. Preheat the oven to 400° F. Combine the egg and water in a small bowl and set aside.

In a Cuisinart® Food Processor, fitted with the medium (4-mm) slicing disc, slice the apple halves using light pressure. Melt the butter in a Cuisinart® 2-quart Saucepan over medium heat. Add the apple slices and brown sugar and sauté until the apples are slightly softened, about 5 minutes. Remove the apples from the heat and allow to cool slightly.

Unfold the pastry sheet onto a lightly floured surface and roll into a 14-inch square. Cut off the corners to make a circle. Place one half of the Brie, cut side up, in the center of the pastry sheet. Top the cheese with half of the warmed apples. Place the remaining Brie, cut side down, on top of the apples. Top the cheese with the remaining apple mixture. Brush the edges of the pastry with the egg wash and fold two opposite sides over the cheese. Trim the remaining two sides to 2-inches from the edge of the cheese. Brush the pastry with the egg wash and fold onto the cheese. Press the edges to seal. Place the Brie and apple pastry seam side down on a baking sheet and brush with any remaining egg wash.

Bake in the preheated oven until golden brown, about 20 minutes. Let the cheese and pastry stand for 15 minutes before serving. Serve with crackers.

Note: We recommend using Pepperidge Farm® Frozen Puff Pastry Sheets.

Nutritional information per serving:
Calories 191 (55% from fat)   carb. 17g   pro. 5g   fat 12g   sat. fat 6g   chol. 31mg   sod. 195mg   calc. 131mg   fiber 2g

CROSTINI WITH FIG & PLUM TAPENADE, SHAVED PARMESAN & FRESH FIGS

A simple yet elegant appetizer that is sure to impress family and friends.

MAKES 24 CROSTINI

24 (1/4-inch)	slices French or Italian baguette (approximately 1 loaf)
4 tablespoons	olive oil
1 teaspoon	kosher or sea salt
1/2 teaspoon	freshly ground pepper

Fig & Plum Tapenade:

3/4 cup	dried figs
1/4 cup	dried plums
1/2 cup	water
1/3 cup	walnuts, toasted
3 ounces	roasted shallots*, quartered
1/3 cup	pitted Kalamata olives, halved
1 tablespoon	capers, rinsed and drained
1 tablespoon	extra virgin olive oil
1 tablespoon	white balsamic vinegar
1/2 teaspoon	herbes de Provence

24	slices shaved Reggiano Parmesan (use vegetable peeler to shave cheese)
12	fresh figs, quartered or sliced
24 (1-inch)	sprigs fresh thyme

Preheat the oven to 350°F. Arrange the baguette slices on 2 large baking sheets and brush the tops with oil. Combine the salt and pepper and sprinkle evenly over the bread. Bake in batches in the middle of the oven until the toasts are pale golden, about 12 to 18 minutes. Cool on a rack. The toasts may be prepared ahead.

Remove the stems from the figs and quarter. Cut the plums in half. Place the dried figs and plums in a small saucepan with water. Bring to a boil, then reduce the heat and simmer until the fruit is tender and the liquid has evaporated, about 5 minutes. Let cool.

Place the walnuts in the Cuisinart® Food Processor fitted with the metal chopping blade. Pulse 10 times to chop the walnuts. Add the softened fruit and any accumulated syrup, the roasted shallots, olives, capers, olive oil, white balsamic vinegar, and herbes de Provence. Pulse 30 to 40 times until the tapenade is a thick, but slightly chunky paste. Let stand 30 minutes to allow the flavors to develop.

Spread each crostini with 1 tablespoon of the Fig & Plum Tapenade. Top with a piece of Parmesan, and 2 fig quarters or slices. Garnish with a sprig of thyme to serve. The crostini are best served shortly after assembling.

°To roast the shallots: Toss the shallots with olive oil and wrap them loosely in foil. Place the foil bundle in a 425°F. oven for 30 to 40 minutes until the shallots are roasted golden brown and soft.

Nutritional information per serving (1 crostini with tapenade, cheese & fig topping):
Calories 126 (35% from fat) carb. 18g pro. 3g fat 5g sat. fat 1g chol. 2mg sod. 177mg calc. 56mg fiber 2g

EGGPLANT CAVIAR

A very unusual and delicious appetizer.

MAKES ABOUT 1 1/4 CUPS

1 1/4 pounds	eggplant, stem end removed
1/4 cup	extra virgin olive oil
3 cloves	garlic, peeled
12 leaves	fresh basil
1 teaspoon	kosher salt
1/2 teaspoon	freshly ground pepper

Insert the thick (8-mm) slicing disc in the Cuisinart® Food Processor. Cut the eggplant to fit the large feed tube. Place the eggplant into the feed tube, and use gentle pressure to slice.

Pour the olive oil into a large Cuisinart® Skillet and heat over medium low heat. Add the garlic and sauté it for about 3 minutes, stirring constantly, until it has browned. Add the sliced eggplant and basil leaves. Cook until the eggplant is softened and lightly browned, stirring often, about 8 to 10 minutes. Season with salt and pepper and let cool 5 minutes.

Place the cooked eggplant in the Cuisinart® Food Processor fitted with the metal chopping blade. Pulse to chop and then process an additional 1 minute.

Serve warm with a toasted bagel or pita chips.

Nutritional information per serving:
Calories 65 (73% from fat) carb. 4g pro. 1g fat 6g sat. fat 1g chol. 0mg sod. 135mg calc. 6mg fiber 1g

CHEVRE & ROASTED PEPPER TARTLETS

Simple to prepare, these savory tartlets will be a hit hors d'oeuvre at your next gathering.

MAKES 24 TARTLETS

3 ounces	cream cheese, cut in 1/2-inch pieces
4 ounces (1 stick)	unsalted butter, cut in 1/2-inch pieces
1 cup	all-purpose flour
1/2 teaspoon	herbes de Provence
1/4 teaspoon	freshly ground black pepper
1/2 (35g)	roasted red pepper, drained and chopped
1 large	egg
5 1/2 ounces	chevre
3 tablespoons	whole milk or half-and-half
1 teaspoon	all-purpose flour
1/4 teaspoon	kosher salt

Preheat the oven to 350° F. Lightly spray 24 mini-muffin cups with cooking spray.

Place the cream cheese, butter, 1 cup flour, herbes de Provence, and pepper in a medium bowl. Mix the ingredients together using the Cuisinart® Hand Mixer using low speed until the mixture forms a ball. Divide the dough into 24 pieces, each about 1 1/2 teaspoons. Roll into balls and use the palm of your hand to flatten these into discs, about 2 1/2 inches in diameter. Press the rounds into the bottom and up the sides of the muffin cups. Spoon about 1/4 teaspoon of the chopped red pepper into each pastry cup. Reserve.

Place the egg, chevre, milk, flour, and salt in the same bowl. Blend with the Cuisinart® Hand Mixer using low speed until smooth and creamy, about 2 minutes. Spoon the filling into the pastry cups, using about 1 1/2 teaspoons per cup.

Bake in the preheated oven for 22 to 24 minutes, until the crust is golden and crispy and the tops are puffed and lightly golden. Let cool in the pan 2 minutes, then gently lift out and cool 5 minutes on a wire rack before serving. These may be made ahead and served at room temperature or slightly rewarmed. (Rewarming in a microwave is not recommended.)

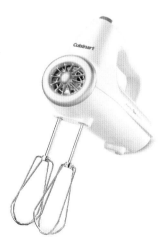

Nutritional information per tartlet:
Calories 98 (71% from fat) carb. 5g pro. 3g fat 8g sat. fat 5g chol. 28mg sod. 97mg calc. 38mg fiber 0g

ENDIVE WITH SHRIMP FILLING

A pretty presentation and delicious too. This is a great finger food,
not too fussy and easy to do ahead of time.

MAKES 24 APPETIZERS

2 tablespoons	fresh parsley leaves
1 small	onion, peeled, quartered
1 tablespoon	vegetable oil
1/2 teaspoon	curry powder
1/4 pound	shrimp, cooked, peeled, de-veined
1/2 cup	cream cheese, in 1-inch pieces
2 heads	Belgian endive

In a Cuisinart® Food Processor fitted with the metal chopping blade, process the parsley until it is finely chopped. Set aside. Place the onion into the work bowl and pulse 10 times to finely chop. Heat the oil in a Cuisinart® 10-inch Skillet over medium heat. Add the chopped onion and cook, stirring, until golden brown, about 8 minutes. Add the curry powder to the onion and cook, stirring, an additional 1 minute. Remove from the heat to cool.

Place the shrimp in the work bowl and pulse to finely chop, about 5 times. Set aside. Process the cream cheese about 15 seconds until smooth. Add the parsley, cooled onion and shrimp. Pulse about 8 times to combine.

Trim 1 inch from the bottom of the endive leaves. Separate the leaves and lay them on a flat serving dish. Pipe or spread the shrimp filling onto the bottom half of the endive leaves. Cover and refrigerate until ready to serve.

Nutritional information per appetizer:
Calories 32 (56% from fat)   carb. 2g   pro. 2g   fat 2g   sat. fat 1g   chol. 14mg   sod. 36mg   calc. 28mg   fat 1g

SIMPLE SALSA CRUDA

Tasty grape tomatoes make this salsa easy to prepare all year 'round.

MAKES 3/4 CUP

1 clove	garlic, peeled
1 tablespoon	fresh cilantro leaves (packed)
1	jalapeño pepper, cored, seeded, cut in 1/2-inch pieces
1	green onion, trimmed, cut in 1/2-inch pieces
1 teaspoon	lime juice
1/4 teaspoon	ground cumin
1 cup (6 oz.)	grape or cherry tomato halves
1/8 teaspoon	kosher salt

Place the garlic in a Cuisinart® Food Processor fitted with the metal chopping blade and process 10 seconds. Stop and scrape the bowl. Add the cilantro, jalapeño pepper and green onion to the garlic and pulse 10 to 15 times. Scrape the bowl again. Add the lime juice, cumin, tomatoes and salt. Pulse 15 to 20 times, until the desired consistency is reached.

Nutritional information per serving (2 tablespoons):
Calories 10 (10% from fat) carb. 2g pro. 0g fat 0g sat. fat 0g chol. 0mg sod. 32mg calc. 4mg fiber 1g

GORGONZOLA-WALNUT SPREAD 🥄

Gorgonzola-Walnut Spread may also be used to stuff hollowed cherry tomatoes as an hors d'oeuvre.

MAKES ABOUT 2 CUPS

2 ounces	walnut halves
2 medium	green onions, white part + 1-inch green
4 ounces	less fat cream cheese
1/2 cup	less fat sour cream
1/4 teaspoon	kosher salt
1/4 teaspoon	freshly ground black pepper
1/4 teaspoon	Tabasco® or other hot sauce
1 1/2 cups	crumbled Gorgonzola

Preheat the Cuisinart® Toaster Oven Broiler to 350°F. Set the rack in the lowest position. Place the walnuts in a pie tin and toast until lightly browned, about 3 to 4 minutes. Cool.

Place the green onions in the Cuisinart® Food Processor fitted with the metal chopping blade and pulse to chop. Remove the green onions and reserve. Place the cream cheese, sour cream, salt, pepper, and Tabasco® in the work bowl, and process to blend until creamy, about 15 seconds. Scrape the sides of the work bowl. Place the reserved green onions, Gorgonzola, and toasted nuts in that order on the creamed mixture. Pulse about 10 times to blend. Transfer the spread to a small decorative bowl and cover. Refrigerate for 1 hour or longer to allow the flavors to blend. If the spread is refrigerated longer than 1 hour, let it stand 10 minutes at room temperature before serving. Serve with crackers, pita chips, or bagel chips.

Nutritional information per serving (2 tablespoons):
Calories 101 (71% from fat)   carb. 2g   pro. 5g   fat 8g   sat. fat 4g   chol. 18mg   sod. 326mg   calc. 116mg   fiber 0g

CROUSTADES WITH ARTICHOKE
AND PROSCIUTTO FILLING

Lower in calories than pastry shells, these crisp and golden-brown toast cups are easy to make and enormously appealing with this delicious filling.

MAKES 36 CROUSTADES

36 slices	thin white bread
1 small	garlic clove, peeled
1/2 small	onion, halved
2 teaspoons	unsalted butter
1/4 cup	parsley leaves
1 1/2 ounces	Parmesan cheese, cut into 1-inch cubes
1 1/2 ounces	prosciutto, cut into 1-inch pieces
2 ounces	frozen artichoke hearts, thawed
2 tablespoons	mayonnaise
	black pepper to taste

Preheat the oven to 350°F. Stack 4 slices of bread at a time and trim the crusts. Place side by side on a cutting board and use a rolling pin to roll the slices very thin. Cut rounds with a 2 3/8-inch cookie cutter (you may use a glass of the same diameter). You will get one round from each bread slice. Reserve the trimmings to use for a bread pudding, stuffing or to grind to make fresh bread crumbs. Fit the rounds into mini-muffin pans° and press into and up the sides of each cup. Bake until golden brown and crisp, about 10 minutes. Remove the Croustades from the oven and reserve. Increase the oven to 400°F.

In a Cuisinart® Food Processor fitted with the metal blade, with the machine running add the garlic through the small feed tube and process the garlic 10 seconds until finely chopped. Add the onion and pulse 8 times to chop. Heat the butter in a Cuisinart® 10-inch Skillet over medium heat and cook the onion and garlic until soft, about 5 minutes. Reserve.

Add the parsley to the work bowl and process 10 seconds to finely chop. Add the Parmesan and process 15 more seconds. Add the prosciutto and pulse 12 times to coarsely chop. Add the onion and garlic, artichoke hearts, mayonnaise and pepper and pulse 6 times to combine.

Fill each Croustade with 1 teaspoon filling and bake until heated through, about 5 minutes. Serve warm.

°Mini-muffin cups measure approximately 1 7/8-inch wide by 3/4-inch deep.

Nutritional information per serving (one filled croustade):
Calories 29 (46% from fat)   carb. 3g   pro. 1g   fat 1g   sat. fat 1g   chol. 3mg   sod. 74mg   calc. 19mg   fiber 0g

Chapter Two

REWARDING SOUPS, SALADS & SANDWICHES

It has been said by many professional chefs that almost any novice cook can prepare a steak, but only a gifted and creative cook can prepare an excellent salad or soup. When you consider the wide variety of ingredients that may be made into a delicious salad or soup, you can understand why the word, "creative" is so distinctively applied. Salads, in addition to being an important part of any healthful diet, can be as simple as a serving of field greens tossed with olive oil and balsamic vinegar, or as complex as a twenty-ingredient mélange of fresh vegetables or fruit with an infused dressing. As an introduction to salads with creative flair, try the recipes that follow in this chapter, such as *Spinach Salad with Grilled Portobellos & Roasted Red Pepper Dressing* or *Avocado and Grapefruit Salad with Lemon Balsamic Vinaigrette.* You'll delight in the fresh change of pace.

Soups hold all the promise of comfort on a cold day and the recipes in this chapter are no exception. The classic choice, *Minestrone,* is well worth the preparation time and has no rival to its rich, full-bodied flavors. *Creamy Onion Soup* begs for only a piece of hearty, peasant bread and a glass of wine to complete a winter's evening meal. Sandwiches such as *Grilled Fresh Mozzarella, Tomato & Basil Panini Sandwiches* and *Veggie Wraps with Guacamole* are especially tempting when paired with these fresh soups or they act as a satisfying entrée when served with a piece of whole fruit or a variety of cheeses.

CAESAR SALAD 🍴

Many people are shying away from Caesar Salad because they are concerned about eating raw eggs. This recipe for the popular salad calls for egg substitute, such as Egg Beaters®, which is pasteurized. Pasteurization eliminates the possibility of harmful bacteria.

MAKES 6 SERVINGS

1 head	romaine lettuce
3 ounces	Reggiano Parmesan cheese, cut in 1-inch pieces
1 large	garlic clove, peeled
4	anchovy fillets
1 tablespoon	egg substitute
2 teaspoons	lemon juice
1 tablespoon	Dijon mustard
2 teaspoons	red wine vinegar
1 teaspoon	Worcestershire sauce
1/8 teaspoon	ground black pepper
1/2 cup	extra virgin olive oil
1 cup	croutons

Clean the lettuce and tear it into 1-inch pieces. Dry the lettuce well and reserve in a large bowl.

Insert the metal blade in the Cuisinart® Food Processor work bowl. With the machine running, drop the cheese through the feed tube and process 30 seconds until finely chopped. Sprinkle the cheese over the lettuce.

In the food processor work bowl, mix the garlic, anchovy fillets, egg substitute, lemon juice, mustard, vinegar, Worcestershire sauce and pepper. Process about 10 seconds until well blended. With the machine running, drizzle the oil through the small feed tube in a steady stream. The dressing will emulsify.

Sprinkle the croutons over the lettuce and add the dressing. Toss to coat and serve immediately.

Nutritional information per serving:
Calories 258 (77% from fat)   carb. 7g   pro. 8g   fat 22g   sat. fat 5g   chol. 12mg   sod. 389mg   calc. 208mg   fiber 2g

BREAD SALAD TUSCAN STYLE

This salad is a creative way to use leftover bread. It is so good, it's worth planning ahead to be sure you have some day-old bread.

MAKES 8 SERVINGS

6 tablespoons	extra-virgin olive oil
2 tablespoons	red wine vinegar
2 cloves	garlic, minced
	salt and freshly ground black pepper to taste
1/2 pound	day-old crusty Italian bread, cut into 1/2-inch pieces (about 4 cups)
5	plum tomatoes, seeded, cut into 1/2-inch pieces
2	seedless cucumbers, peeled, cut into 1/2-inch pieces
2	red onions, thinly sliced
1 bunch	basil leaves, cut into shreds
	shaved Parmesan for garnish*
	extra-virgin olive oil, for drizzling (optional)

In a Cuisinart® Food Processor fitted with the metal chopping blade, combine together the olive oil, vinegar, garlic and salt and pepper for 5 to 10 seconds. Set aside.

In a large bowl mix together the bread, tomatoes, cucumbers, onions and basil. Add the dressing and toss to coat all the ingredients evenly. Serve on a chilled platter or individual plates. Garnish with shaved Parmesan cheese. Drizzle with extra-virgin olive oil, if desired.

Use a vegetable peeler to shave thin pieces from a block of Parmesan. Shave the "curls" only in one direction for best results. Grated Parmesan is a good alternative. The flavor will be the same, although the appearance and texture will be different.

From *Cooking Secrets of The CIA*; adapted by Cuisinart® with permission of the Culinary Institute of America.

Nutritional information per serving:
Calories 168 (31% from fat)   carb. 23g   pro. 7g   fat 6g   sat. fat 2g   chol. 5mg   sod. 238mg   calc. 124mg   fiber 2g

MIXED FIELD GREENS WITH FENNEL, APPLES & LEMON MUSTARD DRESSING

This salad is a nice change in winter. Pears or oranges may be substituted for the apple.
If you wish, slice and add a small red onion to the salad.

MAKES 8 SERVINGS

1 small	shallot, peeled and quartered
2 tablespoons	fresh lemon juice
2 teaspoons	Dijon-style mustard
1/4 cup	extra virgin olive oil
1/4 teaspoon	kosher salt
1/8 teaspoon	ground black pepper
1 large	fennel bulb, halved lengthwise
1 large	firm apple (Gala, Fuji), cored and quartered
1 pound	field greens (mesclun) or baby spinach, washed and dried

With the metal blade inserted in the Cuisinart® Food Processor and the machine running, drop the shallot through the small feed tube and process to chop, 10 seconds. Add the lemon juice and mustard and process another 10 seconds. With the machine running, add the oil in a slow, steady stream, processing until the dressing is emulsified, about 30 to 40 seconds. Add the salt and pepper and process an additional 5 seconds. Pour the dressing into a separate container and reserve.

Insert the thin (2-mm) slicing disc. Trim the fennel to fit the feed tube and using medium pressure slice the fennel and apple. Drizzle with half the dressing. Place the greens in a large salad bowl. Drizzle the greens with the remaining dressing and toss to coat. Add the sliced fennel and apples. Toss gently to combine. Serve.

Nutritional information per serving:
Calories 101 (58% from fat)   carb. 10g   pro. 1g   fat 7g   sat. fat 1g   chol. 0mg   sod. 100mg   calc. 45mg   fiber 2g

SPINACH SALAD WITH GRILLED PORTOBELLOS & ROASTED RED PEPPER DRESSING

Prepare the ingredients for this salad ahead and assemble just before serving.

MAKES 8 SERVING — DRESSING MAKES 1 1/2 CUPS

4 ounces	thick sliced bacon, well chilled
6 tablespoons	extra virgin olive oil, divided
1 tablespoon	freshly squeezed lemon juice
8 ounces	portobello mushrooms, sliced 1/2-inch thick
1 clove	garlic, peeled
1 (1 1/2 oz.)	shallot, peeled and trimmed
1 (6 oz.)	jar roasted red peppers, drained
2 tablespoons	red wine vinegar
2 tablespoons	sherry vinegar
1 tablespoon	light corn syrup
1 teaspoon	kosher salt
1/4 teaspoon	freshly ground black pepper
10 ounces	fresh spinach leaves, washed and dried, tough stems removed

Stack the bacon and cut into 1/8-inch wide slices. Heat a Cuisinart® 10-inch Skillet over low heat and cook the bacon until crispy, 10 to 15 minutes. Drain well and set aside.

Combine one tablespoon of olive oil with the lemon juice and brush on the portobello mushroom slices. Heat a Cuisinart® Grill/Griddle over medium high heat. Grill the portobello mushroom slices until browned and tender, 3 to 4 minutes on each side. Place the grilled portobello on a plate. The bacon and portobello mushrooms may be cooked earlier if desired.

In a Cuisinart® Food Processor fitted with the metal chopping blade, drop the garlic and shallot through the small feed tube and chop for 10 seconds. Scrape the work bowl. Add the roasted peppers, vinegars, corn syrup, salt and pepper and process until smooth, about one minute. Scrape the work bowl again. With the machine running, add the remaining olive oil in a steady stream and process until emulsified, about 30 seconds.

Place the spinach in a large salad bowl and toss with 1/2 cup of the dressing. Arrange the grilled portobello mushrooms over the top. Sprinkle with the cooked bacon bits and serve immediately. Refrigerate any remaining dressing.

Nutritional Information per serving:
Calories 140 (73% from fat)   carb. 4g   pro. 6g   fat 12g   sat. fat 3g   chol. 12mg   sod. 355mg   calc. 25mg   fiber 1g

AVOCADO AND GRAPEFRUIT SALAD
WITH LEMON BALSAMIC VINAIGRETTE

MAKES 8 SERVINGS (2/3 CUP VINAIGRETTE)

1/3 cup	walnut halves
8	grapes
3 tablespoons	fresh lemon juice
1 tablespoon	balsamic vinegar
1/4 cup	extra virgin olive oil
3 tablespoons	walnut oil
1/4 teaspoon	kosher salt
pinch	freshly ground black pepper
10 cups	mixed mesclun greens or other baby lettuces such as arugula, mâche, frisée, radicchio, etc.
2	ruby red grapefruits, peeled, cut into sections
1	Hass avocado, peeled and cubed

Preheat the Cuisinart® Toaster Oven Broiler to 350° F. Arrange the walnuts in a single layer on a baking sheet. Toast the walnuts until golden and fragrant, about 5 to 7 minutes. Remove the walnuts from the oven and allow to cool completely.

Place the grapes in the work bowl of the Cuisinart® Food Processor fitted with the metal chopping blade and pulse 10 times to chop. Add the lemon juice and balsamic vinegar and process until smooth, about 30 seconds. As the processor is running, add the oils to emulsify, about 30 seconds. Season the dressing with salt and pepper.

Place the lettuces, grapefruit slices, and avocado pieces in a large salad bowl. Drizzle with half the dressing and toss to combine. Drizzle with the remaining dressing and garnish with the toasted walnuts. Serve immediately.

Nutritional information per serving:
Calories 186 (73% from fat)   carb. 11g   pro. 2g   fat 16g   sat. fat 2g   chol. 0mg   sod. 48mg   calc. 36mg   fiber 4g

PROVENÇAL WHITE BEAN SOUP

This hearty yet healthy soup can be ready to serve in about 30 minutes.

MAKES 10 CUPS

1 tablespoon	"light" flavored olive oil
1 cup	onions, chopped
1/2 cup	carrots, chopped
1/2 cup	celery, chopped
4 cloves	garlic, peeled
1 teaspoon	herbes de Provence (may substitute dry thyme)
1	bay leaf
5 cups	low-sodium, low-fat chicken or vegetable stock
6 cups	drained cooked white beans (2 (14.5 oz.) cans, rinsed and drained)
2 ounces	lean smoked ham, chopped
1 teaspoon	kosher salt
1/2 teaspoon	freshly ground white pepper
	sour cream and fresh parsley sprigs for garnish

In a Cuisinart® 4 3/4-quart Saucepan, heat the oil over medium heat and cook the onions, carrots, celery and garlic until softened, but not browned, about 3 to 5 minutes. Stir in the herbes de Provence and bay leaf and cook for 1 minute more. Add the stock, drained beans, and ham. Bring to a boil, reduce the heat and simmer, partially covered for 20 minutes.

Remove and discard the bay leaf. Insert the Cuisinart® Hand Blender fitted with the metal blade into the soup. Blend the soup using a slow up-and-down motion until the desired consistency is reached. This will take about 3 to 4 minutes for a smooth textured soup°. Season the soup with the kosher salt and freshly ground pepper.

Serve the soup hot. The soup may be garnished with a tablespoon of sour cream and a sprinkling of chopped fresh parsley.

°If you prefer your soup to have a little texture, shorten the processing time as desired.

Nutritional information per serving (based on 12 servings, without sour cream garnish):
Calories 157 (9% from fat)   carb. 25g   pro. 11g   fat 2g   sat. fat 0g   chol. 1mg   sod. 144mg   calc. 92mg   fiber 6g

CREAMY ONION SOUP

Perfect for a special occasion first course, this creamy soup has surprisingly little cream.

MAKES 8 SERVINGS

2 cloves	garlic, peeled
1 1/2 pounds	onions, peeled, cut in 1-inch pieces
2 tablespoons	unsalted butter
5 cups	chicken or vegetable stock
1	russet potato, peeled and cubed
1 sprig	fresh thyme
1/2 cup	light cream
1 tablespoon	dry sherry
	chopped fresh chives or parsley

Insert the metal blade in the Cuisinart® Food Processor. With the machine running, drop the garlic through the feed tube and chop, 5 seconds. Scrape the sides of the work bowl. Add the onion to the work bowl. Pulse 10 to 12 times to chop.

Melt the butter in 3 1/2-quart Cuisinart® Sauté Pan over medium heat. Add the onions and garlic and sauté until tender and golden, 25 to 30 minutes. Bring the stock, potato cubes and thyme to a boil in a Cuisinart® 3 3/4-quart Saucepan. Reduce the heat to medium low and simmer until the potatoes are tender, 15 to 20 minutes. Stir in the caramelized onions and garlic. Drain the solids from the liquid, reserving both. Remove the sprig of thyme and discard. Let the broth cool slightly.

Place the solids and about 2 cups of the liquid in a Cuisinart® Blender. Blend on high speed until smooth, about 40 seconds. Transfer the smooth soup to a clean saucepan and stir in the reserved cooking liquid, light cream and sherry. Simmer over low heat until heated through.

Serve the soup hot garnished with chopped fresh chives or parsley.

Nutritional information per serving:
Calories 130 (41% from fat)   carb. 15g   pro. 4g   fat 6g   sat. fat 4g   chol. 18mg   sod. 326mg   calc. 38mg   fiber 2g

ASPARAGUS, POTATO & LEEK SOUP 🍳🍳🍳

This fast fresh soup makes a nice first course that will turn any meal into a special occasion.

MAKES ABOUT 8 CUPS

1 pound	asparagus, tough stem ends removed, washed
3 medium	leeks, white and tender green parts only, trimmed, washed*
2 tablespoons	unsalted butter
3 medium	potatoes (about 1 pound), peeled
4 to 6 cups	water
1 teaspoon	kosher salt
1/4 teaspoon	ground black or white pepper
1 cup	fat-free half-and-half

Remove the asparagus tips and reserve. Insert the medium (4-mm) slicing disc in the Cuisinart® Food Processor. Cut the asparagus to fit the feed tube and place them in the feed tube vertically. Using medium pressure, slice the asparagus. Remove to a separate container and reserve. Arrange the leeks in the feed tube vertically and slice.

Place the butter in a Cuisinart® 5 1/2-quart Sauté Pan over medium heat. When the butter has melted, add the leeks and stir to coat with butter. Cover and cook over low heat for 3 to 4 minutes to soften, do not brown.

Insert the shredding disc in the food processor. Cut the potatoes in half crosswise and arrange in the large feed tube. Use medium pressure and shred the potatoes. Add the shredded potatoes and sliced asparagus (still reserving tips) to the leeks with water to cover – about 5 cups. Bring to a boil, reduce the heat to medium-low and simmer until all the vegetables are tender, about 12 to 15 minutes. Stir in the reserved asparagus tips and cook for 3 to 4 minutes. Season with salt and pepper. Stir in the half-and-half and cook over low heat until the soup is hot – do not boil. Serve hot.

* To clean the leeks, remove the root and tough green upper portion of the leaves. Cut the leaves in half lengthwise and rinse under running water. Pat dry or drain before slicing.

Nutritional information per serving:
Calories 73 (25% from fat)   carb. 12g   pro. 2g   fat 2g   sat. fat 1g   chol. 5mg   sod. 131mg   calc. 32mg   fiber 3g

VEGGIE WRAPS WITH GUACAMOLE

A quick "on-the-go" solution for the lunch-time rush.
Cut these wraps into 1-inch thick slices for tasty hors d'oeuvres.

MAKES 4 SERVINGS

2 tablespoons	fresh cilantro
1 small	scallion, trimmed, cut into 1-inch pieces
1/2 small	jalapeño pepper, seeds removed (see note)
1 medium	avocado, peeled, seed removed, cut into 1-inch pieces
1/2 cup	nonfat plain yogurt
1/8 teaspoon	chili powder
1 medium	tomato, cut into 1-inch pieces
5 ounces	Napa cabbage, cut to fit feed tube
2 medium	scallions, cut to fit feed tube horizontally
1 small	yellow pepper, cored, cut into 4 slabs
2 medium	carrots, peeled, cut to fit feed tube horizontally
4 (9-inch)	spinach/garden vegetable flavored flour tortillas

In a Cuisinart® Food Processor fitted with the metal chopping blade, process the cilantro, scallion and jalapeño until finely chopped, about 10 seconds. Add the avocado, yogurt and chili powder and process until smooth, about 10 to 15 seconds. Scrape the sides of the work bowl and add the tomato pieces. Pulse until the tomato is coarsely chopped and combined with other ingredients, about 5 to 6 times. Reserve.

Insert a thin (2-mm) slicing disc and slice the cabbage using light pressure. Transfer the cabbage to a mixing bowl. Place the scallions in the feed tube horizontally and slice. Place the yellow pepper in the feed tube vertically and slice. Add the scallion and pepper slices to the mixing bowl with the cabbage. Insert the medium shredding disc. Place the carrots in the feed tube horizontally and shred. Spoon into the mixing bowl and gently combine the vegetables.

Spread 3 tablespoons of guacamole over each tortilla leaving a 1-inch border around the edge. Arrange 1/4 of the vegetable mixture horizontally across the center of each tortilla, leaving a 2-inch border on the side closest to you. Fold the 2-inch border up and over the vegetable mixture, then fold in the sides and roll up to complete the wrap. Serve the wraps whole or slice in half vertically and arrange on a plate.

Note: Use caution when handling jalapeño peppers. The oils and seeds can irritate your skin and eyes. For best results wear disposable plastic gloves.

Nutritional information per serving (one filled wrap sandwich):
Calories 270 (21% from fat) carb. 46g pro. 9g fat 6g sat. fat 1g chol. 1mg sod. 447mg calc. 148mg fiber 8g

MINESTRONE

Serve along with crusty bread and a green salad for a casual supper. For a meatless version, leave out the sausage and replace the chicken stock with vegetable stock.

MAKES ABOUT 6 QUARTS SOUP, TWELVE 2-CUP SERVINGS

2 tablespoons	extra virgin olive oil, divided
3/4 pound	lean Italian sausage (not in casings)
2 cups	onion, chopped
2 cups	carrots, diced (1/2-inch)
1 cup	celery, sliced
1/4 cup	flat leaf parsley, chopped
4 cloves	garlic, peeled and sliced
1 teaspoon	dried oregano
1 (28 oz.)	can plum tomatoes with juices (dice or lightly crush tomatoes)
8 ounces	yellow squash, cut in 3/4-inch dice
8 ounces	zucchini, cut in 3/4-inch dice
8 ounces	new red potatoes, cut in 3/4-inch dice
1 large	bell pepper (green, red or orange), cut in 1/2-inch pieces
4 cups	low sodium chicken stock
4 cups	water
1 (3 oz.)	piece rind of Reggiano Parmesan cheese (optional)
8 ounces	green beans, trimmed and cut in 1/2-inch lengths (2 cups)
2 (19 oz.)	cans cannellini or white kidney beans
4 ounces	pennette or elbow macaroni, cooked al dente
4 ounces	baby spinach leaves
8	fresh basil leaves, shredded
1 teaspoon	kosher or sea salt
1/4 teaspoon	freshly ground pepper
	freshly chopped parsley leaves
	freshly grated Reggiano Parmesan cheese

Heat one tablespoon of the olive oil in a Cuisinart® 8-quart Stock Pot over medium high heat. Cook the sausage until browned, breaking up with a spatula. Remove the browned sausage and set aside. Discard the fat from the stock pot but leave the flavorful brown bits in the pot. Over medium heat, add the remaining olive oil. When hot, add the onion, carrot, celery, parsley, garlic, and oregano. Cook, stirring for 5 minutes, scraping up the flavorful brown bits while cooking. Add the tomatoes with juices, yellow squash, zucchini, red potatoes, and bell pepper. Cover loosely, and cook over medium low heat for 10 minutes, stirring once or twice while cooking. Add the stock and water to the stock pot, increase the heat to high and bring to a boil. Reduce the heat to low, add the Parmesan rind if desired and cover loosely and simmer for 30 minutes.

After 30 minutes, stir in the reserved cooked sausage, green beans, cannellini beans (do not drain), cooked pasta, spinach, basil, salt, and pepper. Cook until the green beans are tender, about 5 to 7 minutes. Serve the soup hot, garnished with chopped fresh parsley and Parmesan cheese.

Nutritional information per serving (2 cups):
Calories 302 (28% from fat)   **carb.** 39g   **pro.** 17g   **fat** 9g   **sat fat** 3g   **chol.** 19mg   **sod.** 667mg   **calc.** 175mg   **fiber** 8g

GRILLED FRESH MOZZARELLA, TOMATO
& BASIL PANINI SANDWICHES

These delicious grilled sandwiches are a taste of old world Tuscany.

MAKES 2 SERVINGS

4 (1/2-inch)	slices crusty artisan bread* or individual focaccia sliced horizontally
1 tablespoon	extra virgin olive oil
4 ounces	sliced fresh mozzarella (or fresh smoked mozzarella)
4 to 6	thin tomato slices (to fit across bread)
	kosher or sea salt and freshly ground pepper
8 large	basil leaves, shredded

Preheat the Cuisinart™ Griddler™ on high heat. Lightly brush one side of each slice of bread with olive oil. Place two slices on a clean work surface oiled side down. Layer the slices with cheese and tomato and season lightly with salt and pepper if desired. Sprinkle the tomato with the basil shreds. Top with the other slice of bread, oiled side up.

Place the sandwiches on the preheated grill plates and close the griddle. Press down lightly on the top griddle plate for 30 seconds and bake for 3 to 5 minutes. The bread will be grill-marked and crispy and the cheese melted when the sandwich is done. Serve hot.

*You can use plain artisan country bread or a flavored bread such as roasted garlic or rosemary bread, if desired. Slices should be about 7x 3 1/2 x 1/2-inches each.

Nutritional information per sandwich:
Calories 365 (49% from fat)   carb. 29g   pro. 17g   fat 20g   sat. fat 9g   chol. 44mg   sod. 579mg   calc. 9mg   fiber 1g

Chapter Three

AROMATIC BREADS

A h, the scent of baking bread as it wafts through the kitchen—it not only brings you to the table, but it takes you back in time as memories of other kitchens and homemade buttery breads come to mind. The art of baking rolls and breads truly is an art. Because grocery stores stock so many types of bakery goods, we often ignore the pleasure that comes with baking our own rolls and breads, but if you think about how good commercial bread can be, think how much more delicious your own bread will be!

Breads are a great accompaniment to every meal of the day—prepare thick slices of French toast using *French Bread Baguettes*, serve hearty soup with *Focaccia Romana* and try a traditional roast beef with *Roasted Shallot and Rosemary Popovers*. The breads in this chapter offer distinctive ingredients like fresh rosemary, caraway seeds, Asiago cheese, maple syrup and sun-dried tomatoes. Look for the freshest ingredients, including yeast, to make your homemade breads a complete success.

FOCACCIA ROMANA

Impress your friends with this delicious homemade bread.
Focaccia is simple to make in your Cuisinart® Food Processor.

MAKES 18 SERVINGS

2 1/4 teaspoons	active dry yeast (1 packet)
1/8 teaspoon	sugar
1/3 cup	warm water (105°F to 115° F)
4 cups	all-purpose flour
1 teaspoon	salt
1 cup	cold water
4 tablespoons	olive oil, divided
	cooking spray
2 teaspoons	coarse salt

Stir the yeast and sugar into the warm water in a 2-cup measure and let it stand until it is foamy, about 3 to 5 minutes. Place the flour and salt in the work bowl of a Cuisinart® Food Processor fitted with the dough blade and process to combine, about 20 seconds. Add the cold water and 2 tablespoons oil to the yeast mixture. With the machine running (use dough speed if available), pour the liquid through the feed tube in a steady stream as fast as the flour absorbs it, about 35 seconds. Once the dough pulls away from the sides of the work bowl, process an additional 40 to 45 seconds to knead the dough. Place the dough in a lightly floured plastic food storage bag. Let rise in a warm place until doubled in size, about 45 minutes.

Divide the dough in half and roll it into 10-inch rounds. Place the rounds on the baking sheet sprayed with cooking spray. Use kitchen shears to make decorative cuts in the dough. Pull the dough from the edges, opening the cuts to give a lattice appearance. Brush the dough with the remaining olive oil and sprinkle with salt. Cover the loaves with plastic wrap coated with cooking spray and let them rise until puffy, about 20 minutes. Preheat oven to 450° F. Bake the loaves until golden and crisp, about 20 to 25 minutes. Let them cool slightly on wire racks. Serve warm.

Nutritional information per serving:
Calories 129 (23% from fat) carb. 21g pro. 3g fat 3g sat. fat 0g chol. 0mg sod. 279mg calc. 5mg fiber 0g

HERB & CHEESE ROLLS

Serve as warm dinner bread, or let cool and use for sandwiches.

MAKES 16 ROLLS

1 teaspoon	sugar
2 1/4 teaspoons	active dry yeast (1 packet)
1/3 cup	warm (105° F) water
2 cloves	garlic, peeled
2 tablespoons	extra virgin olive oil
4 ounces	aged provolone
2 ounces	Asiago cheese (not grated)
3 1/3 cups	unbleached all-purpose flour
2 teaspoons	Italian herbs (mixed herb blend)
1 teaspoon	dry mustard powder
1 1/4 teaspoons	salt
1 cup	cold water

Combine the sugar, yeast and warm water in a 2-cup liquid measure and stir. Let this stand 5 minutes until foamy.

Insert the metal blade into the Cuisinart® Food Processor. Place the garlic in the work bowl and chop for 10 seconds. Scrape the sides of the bowl. Add the olive oil and process 5 seconds. Remove the garlic oil and reserve. Insert the shredding disc and use medium pressure to shred both cheeses. Remove 1/4 cup shredded cheese and reserve.

With the remaining shredded cheese in the work bowl, remove the shredding disc and insert the dough blade. Place the flour, herbs, mustard powder and salt in the work bowl and process 10 seconds to blend. Scrape the sides of the work bowl. Add the cold water to the yeast mixture and stir to combine. With the machine running (use dough speed if available), add the yeast mixture to flour mixture in a slow steady stream as fast as the flour will absorb it. After the dough forms a ball, process 50 seconds to knead. Transfer the dough to a lightly oiled bowl or re-sealable food storage bag. Cover, seal and let rise, about 45 minutes to an hour, until doubled.

Preheat the oven to 425°F. Divide the dough into 16 equal pieces. Roll each into a 10-inch rope and shape into a knot. Place on a parchment-lined baking sheet, cover lightly with plastic wrap and let rise, about 45 minutes to an hour, until doubled. Brush the tops of the rolls with the reserved garlic oil and sprinkle with the reserved shredded cheese.

Bake for 16 to 20 minutes until the rolls are lightly browned. Remove the rolls to a rack to cool slightly before serving.

Nutritional information serving (1 roll):
Calories 143 (26% from fat)   carb. 21g   pro. 6g   fat 4g   sat. fat 2g   chol. 8mg   sod. 288mg   calc. 91mg   fiber 1g

HARVEST ROLLS

The slightly sweet flavor, golden color and soft texture makes these dinner rolls irresistible.

MAKES 12 DINNER ROLLS

2 1/4 teaspoons	active dry yeast (1 packet)
1 tablespoon	maple syrup
1/4 cup	fat free milk, heated to 110°F-115°F
1/4 cup	frozen cooked squash, drained
2 1/4 cups	all-purpose flour
1/4 cup	sugar
3 tablespoons	unsalted butter, cut into 1-inch pieces
3/4 teaspoon	salt
	cooking spray
egg glaze	(1 large egg blended with 1 teaspoon water)

In a 2-cup liquid measure combine the yeast, syrup and milk. Let this sit until foamy, about 3 to 5 minutes. Stir in squash.

In a Cuisinart® Food Processor fitted with the metal blade process the flour, sugar, butter and salt until combined, about 10 seconds. With the machine running (use dough speed if available), pour the squash mixture through the feed tube in a steady stream. After the dough is formed process until well mixed, about 40 seconds. The dough will be soft and may stick to the sides of the bowl. This is normal. Place the dough in a floured food storage bag and seal the top. Let the dough rise until doubled in size, about 1 hour.

Lightly spray an 8 or 9-inch round baking pan with cooking spray. Punch the dough down and shape it into 12 rolls. Place the rolls, barely touching, in circles in the baking pan. Cover and let these rise 45 minutes.

About 10 minutes before baking place the rack in the Cuisinart™ Convection Oven Toaster Broiler in Position B and preheat the oven to 350°F on the Convection Bake setting. Brush the rolls with the egg glaze and bake until golden brown, about 15 to 18 minutes. Serve warm.

If you do not have a convection model, preheat the oven to 350°F on the Bake setting. Prepare the rolls as directed above and bake until golden brown, about 20 minutes. If the rolls are browning too fast, cover them with foil for the last 5 minutes of baking.

Nutritional information per serving:
Calories 125 (24% from fat)   carb. 20g   pro. 3g   fat 3g   sat. fat 2g   chol. 12mg   sod. 152mg   calc. 16mg   fiber 1 g

FRENCH BREAD BAGUETTES 🥄🥄🥄

This is the quintessential French bread!

MAKES 2 BAGUETTES, EACH ABOUT 12 TO 15 INCHES IN LENGTH

4 cups (15 ounces)	unbleached all-purpose flour
2 1/4 teaspoons	active dry yeast (1 packet)
2 teaspoons	kosher or sea salt
1 1/3 cups	cold water

Insert the dough blade in the work bowl of the Cuisinart® Food Processor. Add the flour, yeast and salt. Process for 10 seconds. With the machine running (use dough speed if available), add the water in a slow, steady stream and process until it forms a ball and cleans the sides of the work bowl. Continue processing for 60 seconds to knead the dough.

With lightly floured hands, carefully remove the dough from the work bowl. Shape it into a smooth ball, sprinkle with flour and place in a resealable 2-gallon plastic bag. Squeeze out the air and seal the bag allowing space for dough to rise. Let the dough rise in a warm place (80° F) until doubled, about 1 to 1 1/2 hours. Punch the dough down in the bag. Remove the dough and divide it into 2 equal portions and let it rest 5 to 10 minutes. Shape each portion into a long, 12 to 15-inch loaf. Place the loaves on a baking sheet lined with parchment or a nonstick baking liner. Cover the loaves with oiled plastic wrap and allow the dough to rise until doubled.

Thirty minutes before baking, preheat the oven to 425° F. Place a 3-quart pan filled with simmering water on the bottom of the oven. Use a serrated knife to make several diagonal slashes 1/4-inch deep across the top of each loaf. Bake on the middle shelf in the oven for 20 to 25 minutes or until well browned. Remove from the baking sheet and cool on a wire rack.

Variation:

White-Wheat French Bread: Substitute 1-cup whole wheat flour for 1-cup all-purpose flour.

Nutritional information per serving:
Calories 153 (3% from fat)   carb. 32g   pro. 5g   fat 0g   sat. fat 0g   chol. 0mg   sod. 224mg   calc. 7mg   fiber 1g

PARMESAN POLENTA ROLLS

These rolls are delicious freshly baked and toasty warm from the oven.

MAKES 16 DINNER SIZE ROLLS.

1/4 cup	yellow cornmeal
3/4 cup	evaporated fat free milk
1 1/8 teaspoons	active dry yeast (1/2 packet)
1/2 teaspoon	sugar
3 ounces	Reggiano Parmesan, cut in 1-inch pieces
1/3 cup	warm water (105°F-115°F)
2 1/8 cups	all-purpose flour
1 teaspoon	salt
4 tablespoons	unsalted butter
5 to 10 drops	Tabasco® or other hot sauce, to taste
	egg wash (1 large egg beaten with 1 tablespoon water)

In a Cuisinart® 1 1/2-quart Saucepan, combine the cornmeal and milk. Heat over medium heat, stirring constantly until thickened. Remove from the heat, cover and set aside for 30 minutes. In a 1-cup liquid measure, dissolve the yeast and sugar in the warm water and let it sit until foamy, 3 to 5 minutes.

In the Cuisinart® Food Processor fitted with the metal blade, drop the Parmesan through the feed tube with the machine running and process to finely chop, about 30 seconds. Leave the cheese in the work bowl and switch to a dough blade. Add the flour, salt and butter and process for 30 seconds to combine. Add the thickened cornmeal and Tabasco®. With the machine running (use the dough speed if your machine has it), add the yeast and sugar through the feed tube in a steady stream as fast as the flour will absorb it. Continue processing until the dough cleans the side of the work bowl and forms a ball. Allow the machine to run for an additional 45 seconds to complete the kneading process. Shape the dough into a smooth ball and place it in a lightly floured food storage bag and seal the top. Let the dough rise in a warm, draft-free place until it has doubled in size, about 45 minutes. Punch the dough down and let it rest 10 minutes.

Lightly spray a 9-inch round baking pan with cooking spray. Divide the dough into 16 equal pieces and shape them into balls. Arrange the rolls seam side down in the prepared pan. Cover loosely with a sheet of plastic wrap and let them rise about 30 minutes. Fifteen minutes before baking, place the rack in Position A and preheat the Cuisinart™ Convection Oven Toaster Broiler to 375° F on the Convection Setting. Brush the rolls lightly with the egg wash. Bake the rolls until they are puffed and golden, about 22 to 25 minutes. Serve the rolls warm. These may be made ahead and reheated.

If you do not have a convection model, place the rack in Position A and preheat the oven to 375° F on the Bake Setting. Prepare the rolls as directed above and bake until puffed and golden about 30 minutes.

Nutritional information per roll:
Calories 127 (34% from fat) carb. 16g pro. 5g fat 5g sat. fat 3g chol. 13mg sod. 195mg calc. 109mg fiber 1g

SWEET POTATO BRAID

This braided bread makes a wonderful addition to any bread basket. It makes great sandwiches, particularly with thinly sliced leftover Lemon Thyme Pork Roast (page 91) and Apple Cranberry Salsa (page 16). For variety, you may shape it into a traditional loaf or into individual rolls.

MAKES 1 LOAF, ABOUT 1 1/2 POUNDS (12 PORTIONS)

1 (8 to 10 oz.)	sweet potato, peeled, cut in 3/4-inch cubes
1 cup	water
2 teaspoons	instant (not rapid rise) yeast
3 cups	all-purpose flour or bread flour
1/4 cup	fat free powdered milk
3 tablespoons	firmly packed light brown sugar
3 tablespoons	unsalted butter, cut in 1/2-inch pieces
1 teaspoon	kosher salt
2 teaspoons	reduced fat milk

Combine the sweet potato cubes and water in a Cuisinart® 1 1/2-quart Saucepan. Cover and bring to a boil. Reduce the heat to low and simmer, covered for 12 to 15 minutes, until the sweet potato cubes are tender. Drain the potatoes, reserving the cooking liquid. Mash the sweet potatoes and measure out 2/3-cup. Reserve the remainder for another use or discard. Measure out 1/3-cup of the cooking liquid and let cool to 105°F to 115° F (check the temperature using an instant read thermometer).

When the liquid has cooled, stir in the yeast until it is dissolved. Insert the dough blade in the Cuisinart® Food Processor. Place the flour, 2/3 cup mashed potato, powdered milk, brown sugar, butter and salt in the work bowl. Process for 20 seconds. With the machine running (use the dough speed if you have it), add the yeast mixture through the small feed tube as fast as the flour mixture will absorb it, about 20 seconds. After the dough has formed a ball, continue processing for an additional 40 seconds. Remove the dough from the work bowl and lightly dust the dough with flour. Place the dough in a resealable food storage bag while pressing out any air and seal. Let it rise in a warm (75°F to 80° F), draft-free place until it has doubled in bulk, about 1 to 1 1/2 hours. Punch the dough down and let rest 10 minutes.

Divide the dough into 3 equal portions. Roll each portion into an even rope about 20-inches long. Lay the strips side by side and braid loosely, pinching the ends to seal them and tuck them under. Place the braid on a baking sheet lined with parchment or a non-stick baking liner. Cover loosely with plastic wrap and let it rise until doubled in bulk, about 1 to 1 1/2 hours.

Twenty minutes before baking, preheat the oven to 375° F. Remove the plastic wrap and brush lightly with the milk. Bake in the preheated oven for 25 to 30 minutes, until evenly browned and hollow sounding when tapped. Transfer the braid to a rack and allow to cool. The braid slices best when it is completely cool.

Nutritional Information per serving:
176 calories (17% from fat)   carb. 32g   pro. 4g   fat 3g   **sat. fat 2g**   chol. 8mg   sod. 123mg   calc. 29mg   fiber 1g

ROASTED SHALLOT AND ROSEMARY POPOVERS

Serve hot popovers with your favorite roast. For plain popovers, omit the roasted shallots and rosemary.

MAKES 12 POPOVERS

5 ounces	shallots, peeled
1 teaspoon	extra virgin olive oil
4 tablespoons	fresh rosemary leaves
1 1/2 cups	all-purpose flour
1 1/2 cups	reduced fat milk
4 large	eggs
3 tablespoons	unsalted butter, melted
1 teaspoon	salt
1/4 teaspoon	freshly ground pepper

To roast the shallots toss the peeled shallots with 1 teaspoon extra virgin olive oil. Place them in the center of a 10-inch square of aluminum foil. Fold the foil loosely to enclose the shallots. Place the foil packet in a preheated 400°F oven and roast until tender and nicely browned, about 45 minutes. Cool the roasted shallots before using.

In a Cuisinart® Food Processor fitted with the metal blade, process the rosemary until it is finely chopped, about 15 to 20 seconds. With the machine running, add the cooled roasted shallots through the feed tube and process 15 seconds. Scrape the sides of the work bowl. Add the flour, milk, eggs, melted butter, salt and pepper and process until smooth, 15 to 20 seconds. Transfer the batter to a large bowl and allow it to rest at room temperature for 30 minutes.

Preheat the oven to 425° F. Spray 12 muffin cups (1/2-cup size) or custard cups with cooking spray. Divide the batter evenly among the prepared muffin tins. Bake in the preheated oven for 40 to 45 minutes. Do not peek or disturb the popovers; they might fall. Remove the popovers from the pans and serve immediately. For a dryer popover, pierce each popover with the blade of a thin, sharp knife after they have been baking 40 minutes. Continue baking for the remaining 5 to 10 minutes.

Nutritional information per popover:
Calories 123 (38% from fat)   carb. 15g   pro. 4g   fat 5g   sat. fat 2g   chol. 79mg   sod. 219mg   calc. 32mg   fiber 0g

OLIVE OIL & ROSEMARY BREAD

Fruity olive oil and rosemary scent this crusty bread.

MAKES ONE LOAF, ABOUT 18 OUNCES

1/3 cup	flavorful extra virgin olive oil
2 teaspoons	dried rosemary
4 1/3 cups	bread or all-purpose flour
2 1/4 teaspoons	sea salt (may use kosher salt)
2 1/4 teaspoons	active dry yeast (1 packet)
1 3/8 cups	warm water (about 105°F)
	corn meal for the baking sheet
	flour for dusting the bread

Combine the olive oil and rosemary, let stand 10 minutes or longer.

Place the flour, salt and yeast in the work bowl of the Cuisinart® Food Processor fitted with the dough blade. With the machine running (use dough speed if you have it), add the rosemary olive oil through the small feed tube in a steady stream. After the olive oil has been incorporated, add the water through the small feed tube in a steady stream, only as fast as the flour will absorb it. After the dough has formed a ball, process for 1 minute longer to knead. Remove the dough from the work bowl, shape into a ball, dust with flour, and place in a resealable food storage bag and seal. Let the dough rise in a warm place until doubled, about 1 hour. Punch down and let it rise again for 1 hour. (This second rise can be skipped if pressed for time, but adds to the flavor and texture of the bread).

Punch the dough to deflate and let it rest 10 minutes. Lightly dust a baking sheet with corn meal. Roll the dough on a lightly floured work surface until it is a rope about 32-inches in length. Join the ends to make an oval or a ring. Transfer the bread to the prepared baking pan and cover with plastic wrap. Let the dough rise at room temperature until almost doubled – about 45 to 60 minutes.

Fifteen minutes before baking, preheat the oven to 450°F. Uncover the loaf and dust with flour. Bake for 10 minutes. Reduce the heat to 375°F and bake for an additional 20 to 25 minutes, until browned and hollow sounding when tapped. Place the bread on a wire rack to cool before cutting. The bread can be warmed again to serve.

Nutritional information per serving (1 ounce):
Calories 136 (31% from fat) carb. 20g pro. 4g fat 5g sat. fat 1g chol. 0mg sod. 170mg calc. 7mg fiber 1g

POTATO CARAWAY STICKS 🥄🥄🥄🥄.

These savory bites can be addictive! Serve as an hors d'oeuvres with cocktails, or as an accompaniment to soup. The recipe can be doubled if you have a 14-cup food processor.

MAKES 10 DOZEN

1 large	baking potato (10 to 12 ounces), scrubbed and dried
1/2 teaspoon	vegetable oil
1 1/4 ounces	Reggiano Parmesan cheese, cut in 1-inch pieces
2 teaspoons	caraway seeds
1/4 cup	unsalted butter, cut in 4 pieces
1 1/4 cups	all-purpose flour
2 teaspoons	kosher salt, divided
1/8 teaspoon	cayenne pepper
1 large	egg, lightly beaten
1 tablespoon	water

Preheat oven to 375° F. Rub the potato with vegetable oil and pierce several times with the tines of a fork. Bake in the preheated oven until tender, about 1 hour. Cut in half and let the potato cool for 10 minutes. Measure out 1 cup of potato flesh; discard the remainder or reserve for another use. Let the potato cool.

Insert the metal blade in a Cuisinart® Food Processor. With the machine running, drop the Parmesan cubes and caraway seeds through the small feed tube and process 15 to 20 seconds, until the cheese is finely ground. Add the cooled potato, butter, flour, 1/2 teaspoon of the salt, and cayenne. Process until the dough just comes together, but does not completely form a ball, about 10 seconds. Shape into a 1-inch thick disc. Wrap the dough in plastic wrap, and chill for 15 minutes in the freezer.

Preheat oven to 475° F. Line baking sheets with parchment or a nonstick baking liner. On a lightly floured surface, roll the dough out to a 1/4-inch thick rectangle. In a small bowl, beat the egg with water to make an egg wash. Brush the egg wash evenly over the pastry surface. Sprinkle the pastry evenly with the remaining kosher salt. Using a pastry wheel or pizza cutter, cut the pastry into 2 1/2 x 1 1/2-inch strips. Arrange the strips 1-inch apart on the prepared baking sheets. Bake for about 12 to 15 minutes until they are golden brown. Transfer the sticks to a rack to cool. These may be served slightly warm from the oven or allowed to cool completely. Store tightly covered in an airtight container.

Nutritional information per serving (4 pieces):
Calories 43 (42% from fat) carb. 5g pro. 1g fat 2g sat. fat 1g chol. 10mg sod. 106mg calc. 17mg fiber 0g

SUN-DRIED TOMATO & PROVOLONE ROLLS

These rolls are delicious when served with supper, or they can be used to make wonderful sandwiches.

MAKES 12 ROLLS

2 1/4 teaspoons	active dry yeast (1 packet)
1/3 cup	warm (105°F to 115°F) water
1 ounce	Reggiano Parmesan cheese, cut into 1/2-inch cubes
6 ounces	extra sharp Provolone cheese, cut to fit the small feed tube
4 cups	bread flour
1 tablespoon	extra virgin olive oil
2 teaspoons	kosher or fine sea salt
1 teaspoon	dry mustard
1 cup	cold water
1/2 cup (3 oz.)	sun-dried tomatoes (not oil packed), roughly chopped

Combine the yeast with the warm water and a generous pinch of the flour in a 2-cup liquid measuring cup and let it stand until foamy, about 5 to 10 minutes.

Insert the metal blade in the Cuisinart® Food Processor. With the machine running, drop the Parmesan cheese through the small feed tube and process 10 seconds to chop. Remove the cheese and reserve. Insert the medium shredding disc and use medium pressure to shred the Provolone cheese. Leave the cheese in the work bowl and insert the metal dough blade. Add the flour, olive oil, salt and dry mustard to the work bowl. Process for 20 seconds to combine. Scrape the sides of the work bowl. Add the cold water to the yeast and stir to combine. With the machine running (use the dough speed if you have it), add the liquid through the small feed tube in a slow steady stream, only as fast as the flour absorbs it. Continue processing until the dough cleans the work bowl and forms a ball. With the machine running, add the chopped sun-dried tomatoes. Process an additional 45 to 50 seconds to knead the dough. Shape the dough into a ball and coat lightly with flour. Place the dough into a resealable food storage bag, press out the air and seal tightly. Put in a warm, draft-free place and allow the dough to rise until doubled in bulk, about 1 hour.

Place the dough on a lightly floured surface and punch down. Divide the dough into 12 equal pieces (about 3.3 ounces/95g each). Let the dough rest 10 minutes. Shape the dough into ovals, about 4-inches in length. Roll each oval in the reserved chopped Parmesan and press in gently. Place the rolls on a parchment lined baking sheet, cover loosely with plastic wrap and let rise, about 30 to 40 minutes, until almost doubled. About 10 minutes before baking, preheat the oven to 425° F. Use a serrated knife to score several diagonal slices on each loaf. Bake for 15 to 18 minutes, until the crust is slightly crispy and lightly browned and the rolls sound hollow when tapped on the bottom. Transfer the rolls to a wire rack to cool. These rolls are best when allowed to cool for 20 minutes before serving.

Nutritional information per serving (1 roll):
Calories 226 (27% from fat) carb. 31g pro. 10g fat 7g sat. fat 3g chol. 13mg sod. 528mg calc. 150mg fiber 2g

Chapter Four

IRRESISTIBLE SIDE DISHES

Garnished with sauces or tossed with herbs, vegetables, fruit, whole grains, rice and pasta contribute to the heart of every meal. Simple side dishes of roasted potatoes drizzled with olive oil and sprinkled with sea salt and freshly ground black pepper adorn an entrée with ease. Roasted mixed vegetables are sweetly rich in flavor.

Each of the recipes in this chapter is prepared using fresh vegetables, herbs and spices. It is particularly important to select vegetables that are at the peak of their season, carefully choosing vegetables that have no blemishes, are firm to the touch without being squishy, have good color overall and smell fresh, not moldy or musty. Herbs and spices deserve equal treatment. If your ground spices are more than six months old, it is time to re-stock your pantry.

Side dishes bring color to your table. Bright green sugar snap peas in *Sautéed Sugar Snaps & Shiitakes*, golden potatoes in *Souffléd Chevre & Green Onion Potatoes* and vibrant multi-colored peppers in *Glazed Vegetables with Fresh Herbs* offer a glimpse of the color and beauty that side dishes bring to your meal.

WILD RICE WITH SHALLOTS AND TOASTED ALMONDS

This hearty dish complements beef, veal and pork dishes.

MAKES 6 SERVINGS

4 cups	water
3/4 cup	wild rice
1 1/2 tablespoons	unsalted butter, divided
1/2 cup	slivered almonds
1/4 cup	fresh parsley
3	shallots, peeled and cut in half
1 rib	celery, peeled, trimmed, cut into 1-inch pieces
1/4 teaspoon	ground black pepper
1/4 teaspoon	salt

Place the water in a Cuisinart® 2 3/4-quart Saucepan. Bring to a boil over medium-high heat. Reduce the heat to low, add the wild rice and simmer, partially covered, until tender, about 30 minutes.

While the rice is cooking melt 1/2 tablespoon butter in a Cuisinart® 3 1/2-quart Sauté Pan over medium heat. Add the almonds and toast, stirring often, until lightly browned, about 5 minutes. Cool slightly.

Place the almonds in a Cuisinart® Food Processor fitted with the metal chopping blade and pulse 6 times to coarsely chop. Remove the almonds and set aside. Place the parsley in the work bowl and process 10 seconds until finely chopped. Remove the parsley and set aside. Place the shallots and celery in the work bowl and pulse 4 to 5 times to coarsely chop.

About 5 minutes before the rice is done, heat the remaining 1 tablespoon butter in the sauté pan over medium heat. Add the shallots and celery and cook, stirring often, until the vegetables are tender, about 3 to 4 minutes. Add the drained rice and the almonds to the sauté pan and cook until heated through, about 3 to 4 minutes. Sprinkle the rice with the parsley and season with pepper and salt. Serve warm.

Nutrition information per serving:
Calories 177 (46% from fat)   carb. 19g   pro. 6g   fat 9g   sat. fat 2g   chol. 8mg   sod. 114mg   calc. 48mg   fiber 2g

SOUFFLÉD CHEVRE & GREEN ONION POTATOES

You can prepare this "soufflé" of mashed potatoes up to a day ahead, making it perfect for entertaining, just cover tightly and refrigerate. Bake about an hour before serving.

MAKES 12 SERVINGS

3 pounds	Yukon gold or russet potatoes, peeled, cut in 1/2-inch slices
1/2 teaspoon	salt
1 teaspoon	white vinegar
8	green onions, trimmed and chopped
1 cup	reduced fat milk
2 tablespoons	unsalted butter
1 teaspoon	kosher salt
5 ounces	chevre
1/2 teaspoon	freshly ground white or black pepper
3 large	egg yolks, lightly beaten
3 large	egg whites

Preheat the oven to 400° F. Lightly butter a 9 x 13 x 2-inch Ceramic Baking Dish.

In a Cuisinart® 3 3/4-quart Saucepan, combine the potatoes with water to cover by 1-inch, 1/2 teaspoon salt and the white vinegar. Bring to a boil, reduce the heat and simmer until the potatoes are tender when tested with a fork, about 18 to 20 minutes. While the potatoes cook, in a separate saucepan, combine the green onions, milk, butter and 1 teaspoon kosher salt. Bring this to a simmer over medium heat, then turn off the heat and let the green onions steep.

Drain the potatoes and place them in a large mixing bowl. Using a Cuisinart® Hand Mixer fitted with the stainless steel beaters, mash the potatoes using low speed until smooth, about 45 seconds. Add the hot milk and onions, chevre, and ground pepper. Mix using medium speed until fluffy, about 50 to 60 seconds. To serve as "regular" mashed potatoes, stop here and transfer the potatoes to a warm serving bowl and serve hot. To make the souffléd version, with the mixer running on low speed, add the beaten egg yolks in a steady stream, beating until totally incorporated.

Place the egg whites in a medium copper, stainless or glass bowl. Beat the egg whites with the Cuisinart® Hand Mixer on high speed until stiff peaks form, about 2 to 2 1/2 minutes. Gently fold the egg whites into the potato/chevre mixture. Spoon the potato mixture into the prepared baking dish . Bake in the preheated oven for 40 to 45 minutes, until the top is pale golden and the potatoes are puffed.

Nutritional information per serving:
Calories 172 (32% from fat) carb. 23g pro. 6g fat 6g sat. fat 4g chol. 65mg sod. 438mg calc. 57mg fiber 3g

SAUTÉED SUGAR SNAPS & SHIITAKES

A nice complement to most any entrée.

MAKES 4 SERVINGS

1 pound	sugar snap peas
2 teaspoons	soy sauce
1/4 teaspoon	brown sugar
2 teaspoons	sesame oil
2 teaspoons	vegetable oil
1/4 pound	shiitake mushrooms, stems removed, wiped clean, thinly sliced
1 teaspoon	sesame seeds, lightly toasted

Remove the strings and tops from the sugar snap peas. Place the peas in a bowl and cover with boiling water and let stand 1 minute. Drain the peas and rinse in cold water. Dry them completely. In a small bowl, combine the soy, brown sugar and sesame oil and set aside. (These steps may be done ahead.)

Heat the vegetable oil in a Cuisinart® 12-inch Skillet over medium high heat. When the oil is hot, add the sliced shiitakes and sauté for 3 minutes. Stir in the sugar snap peas and sauté for 2 minutes longer. Add the soy mixture and stir until the vegetables are coated. Transfer to a warmed serving bowl and sprinkle with toasted sesame seeds.

Nutritional information per serving:
Calories 74 (19% from fat)   carb. 14g   pro. 3g   fat 2g   sat. fat 0g   chol. 0mg   sod. 241mg   calc. 43mg   fiber 3g

GLAZED VEGETABLES WITH FRESH HERBS 🍴

The balsamic vinegar glaze gives a touch of tang to these fresh-herbed vegetables.

MAKES 8 SERVINGS

1/4 cup	loosely packed mixed fresh herbs (parsley, tarragon, thyme, rosemary)
1 (6 oz.)	red onion, peeled, cut in half lengthwise
1	red bell pepper, cored, seeded, cut in 4 slabs to fit feed tube
1	yellow bell pepper, cored, seeded, cut in 4 slabs to fit feed tube
12 ounces	zucchini (1 1/4-inch or less in diameter), cut to fit feed tube
12 ounces	yellow squash (1 1/4-inch or less in diameter), cut to fit feed tube
1 tablespoon	extra virgin olive oil
1/2 teaspoon	kosher salt
2 tablespoons	white balsamic or fruit flavored vinegar
1/4 teaspoon	freshly ground black pepper

Add the fresh herbs to the work bowl of a Cuisinart® Food Processor fitted with the metal blade. Process for 20 seconds to mince the herbs. Remove the herbs and reserve. Insert the medium (4-mm) slicing disc. Use medium pressure to slice the onion and use light pressure to slice the peppers. Remove the vegetables from the work bowl and reserve. Use medium pressure to slice the zucchini and yellow squash. Remove the squash from the work bowl and reserve (do not combine with onions and peppers).

Place the oil in a Cuisinart® 12 1/2-inch Stir-Fry Pan over medium-high heat. When hot, add the onions and peppers, and cook to soften, about 3 to 4 minutes. Add the squash and salt, and cook until tender and lightly golden brown, about 8 to 10 minutes, stirring occasionally. Add the vinegar and continue to cook until the vinegar is reduced to a glaze. Stir in the reserved chopped fresh herbs and the pepper. Serve hot.

Nutritional information per serving:
Calories 47 (33% from fat)   carb. 8g   pro. 1g   fat 2g   sat. fat 0g   chol. 0mg   sod. 170mg   calc. 25mg   fiber 2g

SPINACH STUFFED PORTOBELLOS

Spinach Stuffed Portobellos can be served as a side dish or as a vegetarian entrée.

MAKES 6

6 large	portobello mushrooms, about 4-inches in diameter
2 ounces	Reggiano Parmesan, cut in 1-inch pieces
1 clove	garlic, peeled
1 2 ounce	shallot, peeled
10 ounces	leaf spinach, stems removed, washed and dried
2 tablespoons	sour cream (you may substitute low fat sour cream if desired)
1 teaspoon	Dijon mustard
1/2 teaspoon	kosher salt
1/2 teaspoon	freshly ground black pepper
1/4 cup	pine nuts, lightly toasted

Clean the portobellos with a damp cloth. Remove and reserve stems. Using the bowl of a spoon, scrape out the black gills and discard. Lightly brush the outside of the mushrooms with extra virgin olive oil. Line a large jelly roll pan with parchment.

In a Cuisinart® Food Processor fitted with the metal chopping blade, drop the Parmesan cheese through the feed tube and process 1 minute to chop finely. Add the garlic and shallot and process 30 seconds until finely chopped. Add the mushroom stems and spinach and process 20 to 30 seconds to finely chop. Add the sour cream, mustard, salt and pepper and process until blended. Add the pine nuts and pulse 10 to 15 times.

Preheat the oven to 375°F. Divide the spinach filling evenly among the portobellos, spreading the filling smoothly. Arrange the filled portobellos on the baking sheet and bake until the mushrooms are tender and the filling is hot, about 25 minutes. Serve hot.

Nutritional information per serving:
Calories 117 (44% from fat)   carb. 10g   pro. 9g   fat 7g   sat. fat 1g   chol. 8mg   sod. 327mg   calc. 169mg   fiber 3g

SOUTHWEST PAN ROASTED VEGETABLES

Pan roasting vegetables gives them a hearty, full flavor. Use our Southwest flavors or your own favorites.

MAKES 6 SERVINGS

1/4 cup	fresh cilantro or parsley leaves
2 cloves	garlic, peeled
1	red bell pepper, cored and seeded, cut into quarters
1 medium	onion, peeled and quartered
1 small	yellow squash, trimmed and cut to fit feed tube
1 small	green squash, trimmed and cut to fit feed tube
1 1/2 tablespoons	extra virgin olive oil, divided
2 cups	fresh corn kernels (about 4 ears)
1 teaspoon	ground cumin
1/2 cup	fat free, less-sodium chicken stock or broth
1 1/2 cups	fresh shelled lima beans (may use frozen thawed)
1/2 teaspoon	kosher salt
1/4 teaspoon	freshly ground black pepper
1 to 2 dashes	hot sauce

Insert the metal blade in the Cuisinart® Food Processor. Chop the cilantro for 10 seconds, transfer to a separate bowl and reserve. With the food processor running, drop the garlic through the small feed tube and process 10 seconds to chop. Remove the garlic from the work bowl and reserve. Insert the thick slicing disc. Using medium pressure, slice the pepper and onion, place in a separate bowl and reserve. Use light pressure to slice the squash. Remove the sliced squash from the work bowl and reserve.

Place a Cuisinart® 12 1/2-inch Skillet over medium-high heat and add half of the olive oil. Add the onions, peppers, cut corn and cumin and stir to combine. Increase the heat to high and sauté for 5 minutes. Add the remaining oil, squash and chopped garlic and continue to sauté for 1 to 2 minutes. Add the chicken stock and lima beans and cook 2 to 3 minutes, stirring frequently. Stir in the salt, pepper, hot sauce and reserved chopped cilantro. Serve hot.

Nutritional information per serving:
Calories 163 (23% from fat)   carb. 28g   pro. 6g   fat 4g   sat. fat 1g   chol. 0mg   sod. 183mg   calc. 44mg   fiber 6g

VEGETABLE GRIGLIATA

These grilled vegetables make a beautiful presentation for that special dinner.

MAKES ABOUT 8 CUPS

1/2 cup	extra virgin olive oil
1 tablespoon	fresh rosemary, finely chopped
1 clove	garlic, peeled and finely chopped
1 pound	small eggplant, rinsed
1 teaspoon	kosher salt, divided
12 ounces	red and/or yellow bell peppers, rinsed
12 ounces	yellow or sweet onions, peeled
12 ounces	small zucchini, rinsed
12 ounces	yellow squash or yellow summer squash, rinsed
8 ounces	portobello mushrooms
8 ounces	new red potatoes, steamed to crisp-tender, quartered or halved
8 ounces	plum tomatoes quartered lengthwise
1/2 teaspoon	freshly ground pepper
2 to 3 tablespoons	white balsamic vinegar
1/2 cup	imported or domestic pitted olives, halved
1/4 cup	chopped Italian parsley
1/4 cup	slivered/chopped oil-packed sun-dried tomatoes, drained
1/4 cup	capers, rinsed and drained
1/4 cup	toasted pine nuts (optional)

Combine the olive oil, rosemary and garlic in a small bowl. Let this stand while preparing the vegetables. Cut the eggplant in 1/3-inch slices, sprinkle with 1/2 teaspoon salt and place in a colander to drain. Cut the red/yellow peppers into flat slabs. Cut the onions into 1/3-inch thick slices and slide a toothpick or short wooden skewer into the slice horizontally (this will help to hold it together while grilling). Cut the zucchini and yellow squash into 1/3-inch thick slices. Cut the portobello mushrooms into 1/3-inch thick slices.

Preheat the Cuisinart® Grill/Griddle on High-Sear. Rinse and dry the eggplant slices. Brush all the sliced vegetables lightly with the seasoned olive oil mix — there will be oil mixture leftover. Grill the vegetables on both sides until tender and nicely marked. Eggplant — about 6 to 8 minutes per side; peppers — about 8 to 10 minutes per side; onions — about 5 to 7 minutes per side; squash — about 6 to 8 minutes per side; portobellos — about 4 to 5 minutes per side; potatoes — about 3 to 4 minutes, and the tomatoes — about 1 to 2 minutes. As the vegetables are done, arrange them on a large platter.

Season the grilled vegetables with the remaining 1/2 teaspoon salt and pepper. Drizzle the vegetables with vinegar and garnish with the olives, parsley, sun-dried tomatoes, and capers. Serve warm or cover and refrigerate until ready to serve. Just before serving, sprinkle with toasted pine nuts if desired.

Nutritional information per serving:
Calories 161 (53% from fat)   carb. 17g   pro. 4g   fat 10g   sat fat 1g   chol. 0mg   sod. 540mg   calc. 41mg   fiber 4g

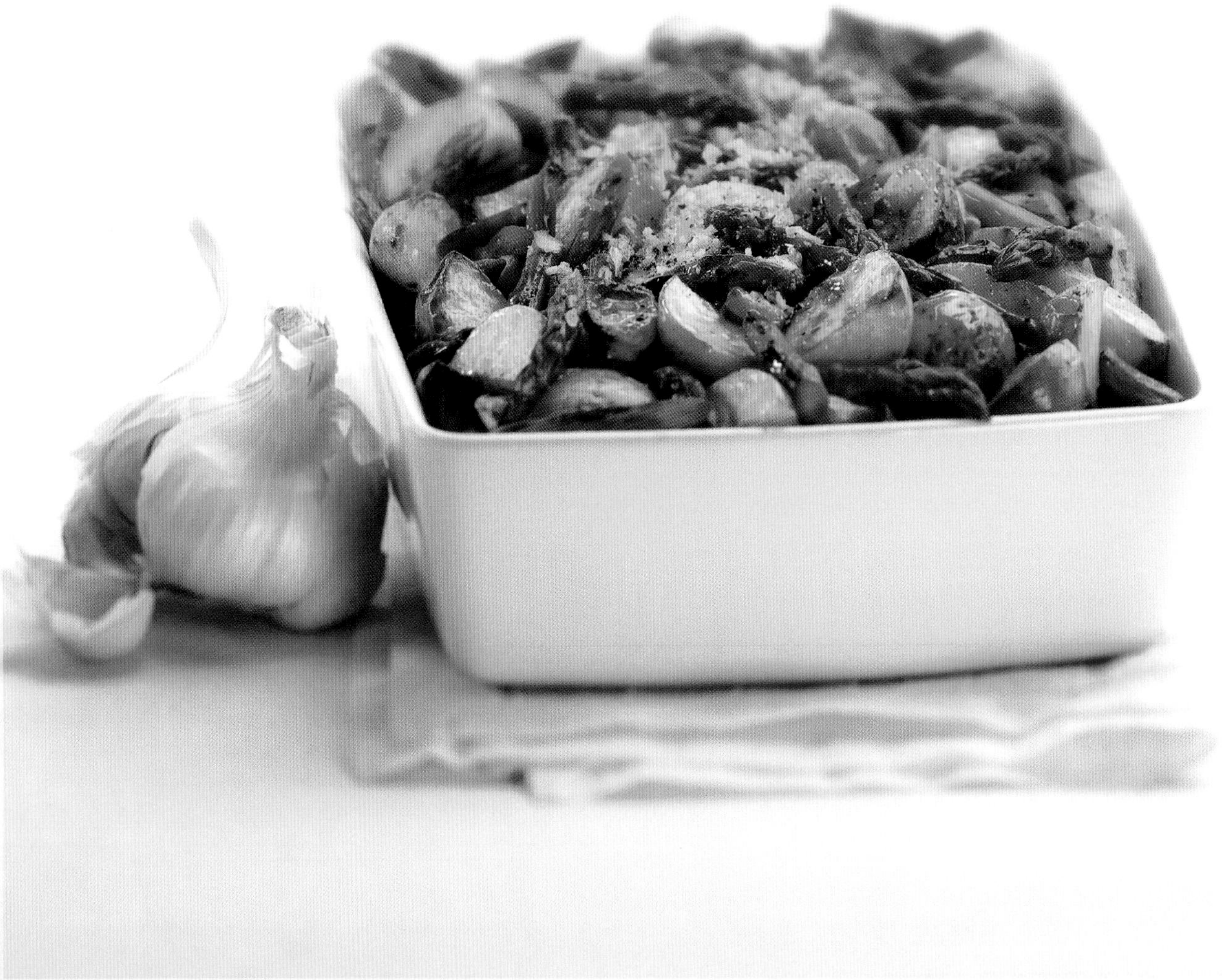

OVEN ROASTED NEW POTATOES & ASPARAGUS 🍴

Our roasted vegetables complement chicken, beef and seafood.

MAKES 6 SERVINGS

1 1/2 pounds	new potatoes (no larger than 2-inches) quartered
8 cloves	garlic, peeled and halved
1 1/2 tablespoons	extra virgin olive oil, divided
1 teaspoon	kosher salt
3/4 pound	asparagus, tough ends snapped off, spears cut diagonally into 1-inch pieces
1/2	lemon zest, bitter white pith removed
1/4 teaspoon	freshly ground black pepper

Preheat the oven to 425° F.

Toss the potatoes and garlic with 1 tablespoon of the olive oil and the salt. Spread the potatoes in a 9 x 13 x 2-inch baking/roasting pan. Cover loosely with a sheet of foil and bake for 15 to 20 minutes. While the potatoes are baking, toss asparagus with the remaining 1/2-tablespoon of olive oil. Place the lemon zest in a Cuisinart® Food Processor fitted with the metal chopping blade. Process 20 to 30 seconds until the zest is finely chopped.

Remove the foil from potatoes and stir. Add the asparagus and continue to bake until both the potatoes and asparagus are tender and browned, about 12 to 15 minutes longer. Just before serving, toss the roasted potatoes and asparagus with the lemon zest and black pepper.

Nutritional information per serving:
Calories 155 (20% from fat) carb. 28g pro. 4g fat 4g sat.fat 1g chol. 0g sod. 230mg calc. 25mg fiber 3g

DELECTABLE ENTRÉES

With thirty recipes to inspire you, this chapter of entrées holds the heart of every meal. Recipes like *Multi-Colored Pasta with Sage & Prosciutto Ricotta Filling for Ravioli, Creamy Parmesan Risotto* and *Lemon Thyme Pork Loin Roast* set the tone for your entire meal and can be as casual as you like or as elegant as the occasion demands. But, don't be fooled into thinking that all of these recipes are difficult. Some have been created specifically to be just as easy to make as they are to enjoy. Many are only moderately difficult and you'll be encouraged by your success when you try them.

When planning your meal, choose the entrée first and build every other dish around it. The recipes in this chapter may encourage you to try some foods you've never tried before, such as *Grilled Swordfish Steaks with Sauce Provençal, Braised Lamb Shanks with Olives* or *Veal Stifado.* Depending on the complexity of your entrée, you will want to partner appetizers, side dishes, salads and desserts to complement and enhance your entrée choice.

Although it is often tempting to ignore the time and attention required by preparing a delicious entrée, you will find that the time you spend in the kitchen gives your family and friends a mealtime that rewards everyone. Diners will want to linger, relax and enjoy each other in your warm atmosphere.

PASTA PRIMAVERA ♨♨♨

This colorful pasta dish is simple to prepare, even after work. The Parmesan and garlic complement the vegetables for a tasty main course.

MAKES 6 SERVINGS

3 ounces	Parmesan cheese, cut in 1/2-inch cubes
2 medium	carrots (4 ounces each), peeled
2 large	zucchini (8 ounces each)
2 large	yellow squash (8 ounces each)
2 large	green bell peppers (6 to 7 ounces each)
2 large	red bell peppers (6 to 7 ounces each)
2 tablespoons	good quality olive oil
2 large	cloves garlic, peeled
1 teaspoon	kosher salt
1/2 teaspoon	freshly ground black pepper
1 1/2 cups	low-sodium, fat-free chicken broth
1 pound	pasta, cooked al dente according to package instructions

Insert the metal chopping blade into the Cuisinart® Food Processor. With the machine running, drop the cheese through the small feed tube and process 20 seconds until finely chopped. Remove the cheese from the work bowl and reserve.

Insert a medium (4-mm) slicing disc into the Cuisinart® Food Processor. Cut the carrots, zucchini and yellow squash to fit the large feed tube. Place the carrots in the large feed tube and slice using firm pressure. Remove and reserve. Using medium pressure, slice the zucchini and yellow squash. Remove the squash from the work bowl and reserve. Remove the stem and seeds from the peppers and cut each into 3 slabs. Arrange the slabs in the large feed tube and slice using light pressure. Set aside.

Heat the oil over medium heat in a Cuisinart® 5 1/2-quart Sauté Pan or Stir-Fry Pan. Brown the whole garlic cloves for about 2 to 3 minutes, turning the garlic over once. Discard the garlic. Add the carrots to the oil and stir-fry for 1 minute. Add the remaining sliced vegetables and the salt and pepper. Stir-fry until just tender, about 4 minutes longer. Add the chicken broth and bring to a boil. Cook until the vegetables are tender, 4 to 6 minutes.

Serve the sautéed vegetables immediately over hot, cooked pasta. Toss to combine and garnish with the reserved Parmesan cheese.

Nutritional information per serving:
Calories 163 (46% from fat)   carb. 15g   pro. 9g   fat 9g   sat. fat 3g   chol. 13mg   sod. 539mg   calc. 210mg   fiber 4g

FRESH YELLOW TOMATO & SCAMORZA PIZZA WITH WHOLE WHEAT PIZZA DOUGH

With a food processor, it's a breeze to make homemade pizza. And, nothing beats the fresh flavor and aroma of pizza baking right in your own oven. Top with your favorite toppings, or try ours.

MAKES ONE 13-INCH PIZZA, 4 SERVINGS

	Whole Wheat Pizza Dough (recipe follows)
	extra virgin olive oil
6 to 8 ounces	scamorza* cheese
5 ounces	red onion, peeled and ends cut flat
12 ounces	fresh yellow tomatoes, stem end cut flat
24 leaves	fresh oregano

Preheat the oven to 500°F. Roll the pizza dough out into a 13-inch round and brush generously with olive oil. Place the dough on a perforated pizza pan or pizza screen. The pizza may also be baked on a baking stone following the manufacturer's instructions.

Insert the medium (4-mm) slicing disc in the Cuisinart® Food Processor. Place the cheese in the large feed tube and slice using medium pressure. Remove the cheese and reserve. Place the onion in the large feed tube and with medium pressure, slice. Remove and reserve. Place the tomatoes in the large feed tube, cut side down, and use light pressure to slice. Remove the tomatoes and reserve.

Arrange the slices of tomato and cheese on top of the prepared dough. Top with the onion slices and half of the oregano leaves. Bake in the preheated oven until the dough is crisp and the topping is golden brown. Remove the pizza from the oven and garnish with the remaining oregano leaves.

*Scamorza is similar to mozzarella…creamy white in color with a slightly nutty flavor. Scamorza is firmer and has a little less moisture than mozzarella which makes it perfect to slice as a topping for pizza.

Whole Wheat Pizza Dough, page 82

WHOLE WHEAT PIZZA DOUGH

2 1/4 teaspoons	active dry yeast (1 packet)
1 teaspoon	sugar
2/3 cup	warm water (105°F to 115° F)
1/2 teaspoon	salt
1/2 cup	whole wheat flour
1 cup	all-purpose flour
2 tablespoons	extra-virgin olive oil

Stir the yeast and sugar into the warm water and let it stand for 5 to 10 minutes.

Process the salt and flours with the metal blade of the Cuisinart® Food Processor until combined, about 30 seconds. Add the oil to the yeast mixture. With the motor running, pour the yeast and oil through the feed tube in a steady stream as fast as the flour absorbs it, about 30 seconds. Process until the dough forms a ball, adding flour by the tablespoon if the dough seems too sticky. Process an additional 45 seconds to knead the dough. Pat the dough into a large ball.

For one 13-inch pizza, use all the dough. For 8-inch individual pizzas, use 1/3 cup dough for each. Roll the dough out very thinly on a lightly floured surface. Place the dough in an oiled 13-inch black steel pizza pan or on two oiled baking sheets.

Layer the pizza toppings on the dough as directed above and bake according to the directions.

Nutritional information per serving:
Calories 429 (46% from fat)   carb. 44g   pro. 15g   fat 22g   sat. fat 7g   chol. 33mg   sod. 464mg   calc. 244mg   fiber 4g

BAKED STUFFED PORK CHOPS

The fruit and nut stuffing compliments the delicious pork flavor.

MAKES 4 SERVINGS

2/3 cup	pecan halves
	cooking spray
2/3 cup	dried pitted apricots
2 tablespoons	apricot preserves
1 teaspoon	Dijon-style mustard
4	boneless loin pork chops, about 1-inch thick
	salt and pepper to taste

Place the rack in Cuisinart® Toaster Oven Broiler in position B and preheat the oven to 325° F on the Bake setting. Arrange the pecan halves in a baking pan in a single layer. Bake in the preheated oven until fragrant, about 8 to 10 minutes. Remove the toasted pecans and allow to cool slightly.

Place the broiling rack in the baking pan on the lower position and lightly coat the broiling rack with cooking spray. Increase the oven temperature to 375° F. Place the toasted pecans and apricots in a Cuisinart® Food Processor fitted with the metal chopping blade. Process 15 to 20 seconds until the fruit and nuts are coarsely chopped. Add the apricot preserves and mustard to the work bowl and pulse until combined.

Use a sharp pointed knife to make a 3-inch slit in each pork chop. Make the inside pocket on the pork chop larger than the slit. Season the pork chops with salt and pepper. Stuff each pork chop with 2 to 3 tablespoons of the apricot and pecan stuffing.

Arrange the pork chops in a single layer on the prepared broiling rack. Bake for 20 minutes, turn each chop over and bake until the juices are clear and the meat is no longer pink, about 20 minutes longer. The internal temperature of the meat should be 165° F. Set the oven to Broil setting. Broil, keeping the door ajar, until the tops of the pork chops are golden brown. Serve immediately.

Nutritional information per serving:
Calories 534 (45% from fat)   carb. 22g   pro. 52g   fat 27g   sat. fat 6g   chol. 125mg   sod. 305mg·   calc. 30mg   fiber 4g

CHICKEN STIR FRY WITH CASHEWS

Pan-Asian and Mexican flavors unite to create this wonderful dish.
Shrimp or pork may be substituted for the chicken.

MAKES 6 SERVINGS

4	boneless, skinless chicken breast halves
1 garlic	clove, peeled
1 (1-inch)	piece ginger root, peeled
1/4 cup	fresh cilantro
1 pound	jicama, peeled, cut to fit feed tube
2 medium	carrots, peeled, cut to fit feed tube horizontally
4 medium	scallions, trimmed, cut to fit feed tube vertically
1 medium	red bell pepper, cored, cut into 4 slabs
1 tablespoon	vegetable oil
1/2 cup	canned baby corn, drained
1/2 cup	bottled stir fry sauce
1/2 cup	cashews

Place each chicken breast half on a piece of plastic wrap. Tuck the ends of the breasts under to form a uniform thickness and roll each piece up in plastic wrap to seal. Freeze the chicken breasts until firm to the touch but easily pierced with the tip of a sharp knife.

In a Cuisinart® Food Processor fitted with the metal chopping blade, process the garlic and ginger for 5 seconds until finely minced. Remove the garlic and ginger from the work bowl and reserve. Place the cilantro in the work bowl and process 5 seconds until it is finely chopped. Remove the cilantro and reserve. Insert the French Fry-Cut disc. Process the jicama using medium pressure. Place the jicama in a mixing bowl. Insert the shredding disc and shred the carrots using medium pressure. Spoon the carrots into the bowl with the jicama. Insert the medium (4-mm) slicing disc and slice the scallions and red pepper. Place these in the bowl with the jicama. Cut the chicken breasts in half vertically and place them in the feed tube cut side down and slice using medium pressure.

Preheat the Cuisart™ Electric Wok to 350°F. Add the vegetable oil and stir fry the garlic and ginger until golden brown, about 1 to 2 minutes. Add the chicken and stir fry until it is no longer pink, about 4 to 5 minutes. Add the jicama, carrots, scallions and peppers and stir fry until crisp-tender, about 2 to 3 minutes. Add the baby corn and cook 1 minute longer. Add the stir-fry sauce and stir until well mixed and heated through. Turn the wok off. Sprinkle the stir-fry with cilantro and cashews and stir. Serve immediately over white or brown rice.

Nutritional information per serving:
Calories 247 (31% from fat)   carb. 17g   pro. 27g   fat 9g   sat. fat 2g   chol. 64mg   sod. 836mg   calc. 34mg   fiber 3g

CAJUN EYE ROUND ROAST 🍴🍴🍴

Full of flavor, but not too spicy hot. Thinly slice leftovers to make great sandwiches.

MAKES 8 6-OUNCE SERVINGS

4 tablespoons	sweet paprika
1 1/2 tablespoons	kosher salt
1 tablespoon	sugar
1	bay leaf, roughly broken
1 tablespoon	garlic powder
1 tablespoon	minced dry onions
1 tablespoon	freshly ground black pepper
1/2 to 1 tablespoon	cayenne pepper
1 tablespoon	dry oregano
2 teaspoons	dry thyme
1 1/2 teaspoons	dry basil
1 teaspoon	dry rosemary
1/2 teaspoon	ground allspice
3 pound	eye of round roast

In a Cuisinart® Food Processor fitted with the metal chopping blade, combine the first thirteen ingredients. Process on high speed for 20 to 30 seconds until there are no visible pieces of the bay leaf. This makes 3/4 cup (4 ounces) of Cajun Spice Rub. Transfer the rub to a jar with a tight fitting lid for storage.

Rub the eye of round with 1 1/2 tablespoons of Cajun Spice Rub. Lightly coat the rack of the broiler pan of the Cuisinart® Toaster Oven Broiler with cooking spray. Arrange the seasoned roast on the rack and allow it to rest for 30 minutes at room temperature. You may season the roast up to a day ahead by wrapping it loosely in waxed paper and storing it in the coolest part of the refrigerator until ready to use. Allow the roast to temper for 30 minutes at room temperature before roasting. Place the rack in the Cuisinart® Toaster Oven Broiler in Position B and preheat the oven to 450° F on Convection Bake Setting.

Place the roast in the Cuisinart® Toaster Oven Broiler and reduce the heat to 350°F, still on the Convection setting. Roast for about 45 minutes, until the meat thermometer registers 130° F in the center. Remove the roast from the oven and loosely tent it with foil and let it rest for 10 to 20 minutes (the internal temperature will rise another 10 to 15 degrees as the meat rests, and will be medium-rare) before slicing. Slice thinly to serve.

If your Toaster Oven Broiler does not have the Convection setting, use Bake setting. Follow the above directions and increase the cooking time to 55 to 65 minutes. Allow the meat to rest before slicing. Slice thinly to serve.

Nutritional information per serving (6-ounce):
Calories 221 (31% from fat)   carb. 1g   pro. 36g   fat 7g   sat.fat 3g   chol. 86mg   sod. 171mg   calc. 11mg   fiber 0g

GRILLED SWORDFISH STEAKS 𝄞𝄞𝄞 WITH SAUCE PROVENÇAL

Inclement weather is not a problem with our Grill Pan.

MAKES 4 SERVINGS

2	leeks, trimmed, washed and dried
2 small cloves	garlic, peeled
3 tablespoons	freshly squeezed lemon juice
3 tablespoons	extra virgin olive oil, divided
1 1/2 teaspoons	Dijon mustard
1/2 teaspoon	kosher salt
1/2 teaspoon	freshly ground black pepper
4	swordfish steaks, about 6 ounces each (3/4-inch thick)
1 (15 oz.)	can diced tomatoes, drained
1/3 cup	dry white wine or vermouth
12	fresh basil leaves
16	imported black olives (such as Kalamata), pitted and quartered

In a Cuisinart® Food Processor fitted with the medium (4-mm) slicing disc, slice the leeks using medium pressure. Remove the leeks from the work bowl and reserve. Insert the metal blade and drop the garlic through the feed tube and process about 10 seconds to chop finely. Scrape the sides of the work bowl and set aside in a separate bowl half of the garlic. Add the lemon juice, two tablespoons of the olive oil, mustard, and half the salt and pepper to the work bowl.

Process 10 seconds. Arrange the swordfish in a flat dish and pour the lemon-mustard marinade over it. Allow the fish to marinate at room temperature for 20 to 30 minutes.

In a 2-quart Cuisinart® Sauté Pan, heat the remaining olive oil over medium high heat. Add the reserved chopped garlic and sliced leeks. Cook for 5 to 10 minutes until the leeks are softened. Stir in the tomatoes and wine and cook over medium heat until thickened, about 10 minutes. (This sauce may be prepared ahead of time. Just refrigerate the sauce and reheat when ready to continue.) While the sauce is cooking, stack the basil leaves, roll, and cut into very thin slices with a sharp knife. When the sauce has thickened, stir in the remaining salt and pepper. Keep the sauce warm over very low heat.

Preheat a Cuisinart® Grill/Griddle on medium high heat. When the grill is hot, arrange the swordfish on the grill pan and grill for 5 to 6 minutes per side. Transfer the grilled fish to a warmed platter or plates. Stir the shredded basil and quartered olives into the simmering sauce and just heat the olives through, about 1 minute. Serve the sauce with the grilled swordfish.

Variation:

Use tuna steaks in place of swordfish steaks.

Nutritional information per serving:
Calories 407 (444% from fat) carb. 13g pro. 42g fat 20g sat. fat. 3g chol. 73mg sod. 1167mg calc. 58mg fiber 5g

HEARTY TURKEY CHILI WITH BLACK BEANS 🍴🍴🍴

Turkey breast makes this chili low fat and heart healthy.
If you prefer beef, use well-trimmed lean beef chuck or round.

MAKES 8 SERVINGS

2 cloves	garlic, peeled
2 (4 oz.)	onions, peeled and cut in 1-inch cubes
1 1/2 pounds	boneless, skinless, turkey breast, cut in 1-inch cubes, well-chilled
1 tablespoon	olive oil
2 tablespoons	chili powder
1 tablespoon	ground cumin
1 teaspoon	ground cinnamon
1/2 teaspoon	ground coriander
2 (15 oz.)	cans diced tomatoes with juice
1 1/2 cups	water
1 teaspoon	kosher salt
2 (15 oz.)	cans black beans, drained, rinsed and drained again

In a Cuisinart® Food Processor fitted with the metal blade, process the onions and garlic using pulse until finely chopped, about 15 to 20 times. Remove the onions and garlic to a separate bowl and reserve. In two or more batches, depending on the size of the machine, process the turkey cubes until coarsely chopped, about 10 to 15 pulses. Carefully wash the work surface and your hands with soap and hot water.

Heat the oil in a Cuisinart® 6-quart Sauce Pot over medium heat and quickly cook the chopped onions and garlic until tender and translucent, about 3 to 4 minutes. Stir in the ground turkey and cook, stirring often, until lightly browned and no longer pink, 5 to 10 minutes. Add the chili powder, cumin, cinnamon and coriander and cook uncovered for 5 minutes. Stir in the tomatoes with their juices, water and salt. Cover the pot loosely and let the chili simmer for 3 hours, stirring occasionally. Stir in the beans and cook until heated through. Taste the chili and adjust the seasonings as needed. The chili may be prepared a day ahead and reheated. If preparing the chili to freeze, do not add the beans until the chili is thawed and reheated. The chili may be served with shredded cheddar or Monterey Jack cheeses, sliced jalapeño peppers, chopped red/green peppers, chopped scallions, sliced black olives, chopped tomato, chopped avocado and sour cream.

Nutritional information per serving:
Calories 275 (17% from fat)   carb. 30g   pro. 29g   fat 5g   **sat. fat 1g**   chol. 51mg   sod. 371mg   calc. 74mg   fiber 11g

CHICKEN WITH TARRAGON MUSHROOM SAUCE 🥄🥄🥄

An elegant entrée that is perfect for a special occasion.

MAKES 6 SERVINGS

6	boneless skinless chicken breast halves (about 5 ounces each)
4	green onions, trimmed and cut into 1-inch pieces
1/2 cup	fresh flat parsley leaves
8 ounces	mushrooms, cleaned
2 tablespoons	unsalted butter, divided
1 tablespoon	extra virgin olive oil
2 teaspoons	dried tarragon (you may substitute 4 teaspoons fresh chopped tarragon)
3/4 cup	dry white wine or vermouth
1/2 cup	low sodium, low fat chicken broth
1/2 teaspoon	kosher salt
1/4 teaspoon	freshly ground black pepper
1/4 cup	half & half

One at a time, place each chicken breast half between 2 sheets of plastic wrap. Pound each breast with a flat pounder to an even thickness, about 1/2-inch. Set aside. Wash your hands and work surface with soap and hot water.

In a Cuisinart® Food Processor fitted with the metal chopping blade, place the green onions and parsley in the work bowl. Pulse 5 times to chop. Scrape the work bowl and pulse 5 to 10 seconds to finely chop. Insert the medium (4-mm) slicing disc and using light pressure slice the mushrooms. Remove the mushrooms and herbs and reserve.

Place a Cuisinart® 5 1/2-quart Sauté Pan over medium high heat and add half the butter and all the olive oil. Swirl the pan to distribute the bubbling butter and oil evenly. Sauté the chicken breast halves until golden on each side, about 3 to 4 minutes per side. Remove the chicken breasts to a plate and cover loosely with foil. Add the remaining butter to the pan. When melted, add the reserved mushrooms and herbs. Cook over medium high heat until the mushrooms start to become golden on the edges, about 4 to 5 minutes. Stir in the tarragon and add the vermouth and chicken broth. Continue cooking, scraping the brown bits from the bottom of the pan and reduce the liquid by half. Return the chicken and any accumulated juices to the pan and cook for 3 to 4 minutes. Stir in the salt, pepper and half & half.

Transfer the chicken to a warmed platter. Cook the mushroom mixture over medium high heat for 2 to 3 minutes to thicken. Spoon the sauce over the chicken and garnish with sprigs of fresh tarragon if desired. Serve warm.

Nutritional information per serving:
Calories 238 (33% from fat)   carb. 4g   pro. 32g   fat 9g   sat. fat 4g   chol. 94mg   sod. 542mg   calc. 53ng   fiber 1g

SAUTÉ OF CHICKEN WITH FENNEL AND APPLES

Serve with the mashed version of Souffléd Chevre & Green Onion Potatoes (page 66), or your favorite mashed potatoes.

MAKES 4 SERVINGS

2 tablespoons	chopped Italian parsley
2 cloves	garlic, minced
1 large	fennel bulb, 1 1/4 to 1 1/2 pounds, trimmed to fit large feed tube
1 large	Golden Delicious apple, about 1/2 pound, cored and halved
4	boneless, skinless chicken breast halves, about 5 ounces each
1/2 teaspoon	kosher salt, divided
1/4 teaspoon	freshly ground black pepper, divided
2 tablespoons	extra virgin olive oil, divided
2 teaspoons	herbes de Provence
1/2 cup	chicken stock

In a Cuisinart® Food Processor fitted with the metal chopping blade, process the parsley for 10 seconds to chop. Remove the parsley to a separate bowl and reserve. With the machine running, drop the garlic through the feed tube and process 10 seconds to chop. Remove the garlic and reserve. Insert the medium (4-mm) slicing disc and use medium pressure to slice the fennel and apples. Remove and reserve.

Place the chicken between two sheets of plastic wrap and use a flat meat pounder to pound to an even thickness of 1/2-inch. Season the chicken with 1/4 teaspoon of the salt and 1/8 teaspoon of the pepper.

In a Cuisinart® 5 1/2-quart Sauté Pan, heat one tablespoon of the oil over medium high heat. Add the fennel, apples, herbs and the remaining 1/4 teaspoon of salt and 1/8 teaspoon of pepper. Cook for 10 to 12 minutes, stirring now and then until the fennel and apples are tender and golden brown. Transfer to a dish and cover loosely with foil.

With the sauté pan still over medium high heat, add the remaining olive oil and heat. Add the chicken to the pan skin side down and sprinkle with the remaining herbs. Cook for about 5 minutes. Stir in the garlic, turn the chicken and cook for 3 to 4 minutes longer. Remove the chicken from the pan and keep warm with the fennel and apples. Add the chicken stock to the pan and cook for 1 minute to reduce by half. Return the chicken, fennel and apples, and any accumulated juices to the pan. Bring to a simmer. Cover and remove the pan from the heat and let it sit for 5 minutes to steam. Sprinkle the chicken with the reserved parsley and serve hot.

Nutritional information per serving:
Calories 264 (27% from fat) carb. 18g   pro. 32g   fat 8g   sat. fat 1g   chol. 79mg   sod. 668mg   calc. 90mg   fiber 2g

LEMON THYME PORK LOIN ROAST 🥄🥄🥄

Serve with Apple Cranberry Salsa (page 16) for something just a little different.

MAKES 12 SERVINGS

1 (3 pound)	boneless pork loin roast, (about 10 to 12 inches in length)
1 tablespoon	extra virgin olive oil
1 tablespoon	balsamic vinegar
4 strips	lemon zest (2 x 1/2-inches, about the zest of 1/2 lemon), bitter white pith removed
3 cloves	garlic, peeled
1 teaspoon	kosher salt
1 teaspoon	thyme (you may use 2 to 3 teaspoons of fresh thyme leaves if desired)
1/2 teaspoon	black peppercorns

Tie the pork roast with butcher's twine at 1-inch intervals to help it maintain a round shape for even cooking (a butcher will also be able to do this for you). The pork roast should be approximately 12-inches in length, not doubled and tied. Rub the roast with the oil and vinegar.

Place the lemon zest, garlic, kosher salt, thyme and peppercorns in the work bowl of the Cuisinart® Food Processor. Process for 10 seconds. Scrape the work bowl and process again for 5 to 10 seconds or longer, until the mixture resembles a coarse paste. Rub the paste evenly all over the surface of the roast. The meat may be roasted immediately or covered loosely with waxed paper, and refrigerated for up to 8 hours (the longer the rub is on the meat, the more intense the flavor will be). If refrigerated for longer than 1 hour, take the meat out of the refrigerator 20 to 30 minutes before roasting.

Arrange the rack in Position A and preheat the Cuisinart® Toaster Oven Broiler to 450°F. Arrange the rack in the drip pan in the upper-most position and coat lightly with cooking spray. Center the roast on the rack and roast in the oven for 15 minutes. Decrease the heat to 325° F and continue roasting for an additional 35 to 45 minutes, until a meat thermometer inserted in the center of the roast registers 155° F to 160° F. Turn off the oven and transfer the roast to a warm platter. Let the roast rest for 10 minutes before slicing. Carve the roast into slices 1/4-inch thick or less, as preferred.

Nutritional information per serving:
Calories 239 (37% from fat) carb. 1g pro. 35g fat 9g sat. fat 3g chol. 87mg sod. 165mg calc. 5mg fiber 0g

PAN ROASTED SHRIMP AND SCALLOPS
WITH CREAMY SPINACH FETA SAUCE OVER FARFALLE

Turn this into a vegetarian entrée by substituting
6 portobello mushrooms cut into one-half inch thick slices for the seafood.

MAKES 6 SERVINGS

1 clove	garlic, peeled
1 medium	onion (5 to 6 ounces), peeled, cut into 1-inch pieces
1 1/2 tablespoons	extra virgin olive oil, divided
1 teaspoon	dry oregano
1 (10 oz.)	package frozen chopped spinach, thawed, squeezed dry
3/4 cup	fat free evaporated milk
3/4 cup	chicken stock
4 ounces	feta cheese, crumbled
1 tablespoon	fresh lemon juice
12 ounces	farfalle pasta
1 tablespoon	unsalted butter
8 ounces	extra large shrimp, peeled and deveined
8 ounces	sea scallops, tough "foot" removed

Insert the metal chopping blade in a Cuisinart® Food Processor. With the machine running, drop the garlic through the feed tube and process for 10 seconds. Scrape the sides of the work bowl. Add the onion and pulse 10 to 15 times to chop. In a Cuisinart® 3-quart Sauté Pan, heat 1/2 tablespoon of the oil over medium low heat. Add the onions and garlic and cook until tender and translucent, 3 to 4 minutes, do not brown. Add the oregano and spinach and cook for 2 to 3 minutes. Stir in the evaporated milk, stock, 3/4 of the feta cheese and lemon juice. Simmer for 5 minutes over medium-low heat, stirring, until thickened and the cheese is melted. Transfer the sauce to the food processor and process until smooth. Return the sauce to the pan and keep warm over low heat.

Bring salted water to a boil in a Cuisinart® Stock Pot. Cook the pasta according to package directions. When the pasta is nearly cooked, heat the remaining oil with the butter in a Cuisinart® 12 1/2-inch Skillet over medium-high heat. When the foaming from the butter subsides, add the shrimp and scallops in a single layer and cook until golden, about 2 to 3 minutes. Drain and discard any accumulated liquid before turning the shrimp and scallops to cook the other side. Season the seafood with salt and freshly ground pepper. Drain the pasta, reserving 1/2 cup of the pasta cooking water. Add the drained pasta to the sauce in the pan. Stir in as much of the reserved pasta cooking water as needed if the sauce is too thick. Transfer the pasta and sauce to a warm platter and top with the cooked shrimp and scallops. Garnish with the remaining feta cheese.

Nutritional information per serving:
Calories 429 (25% from fat)   carb. 54g   pro. 21g   fat 11g   sat. fat 4g   chol. 108mg   sod. 489mg   calc. 293mg   fiber 4g

MIXED MUSHROOM RAGOUT WITH PENNE

This hearty, delicious yet healthy pasta is sure to please.

MAKES 8 SERVINGS

1/2 cup	fresh Italian parsley leaves, washed and dried
1 to 2 cloves	garlic, peeled
1 (6 oz.)	onion, peeled, cut into 1-inch cubes
3/4 pound	cremini or white mushrooms, cleaned
1/2 pound	portobello mushrooms, cleaned
1/4 pound	shiitake mushrooms, cleaned, tough stems removed
1/4 pound	oyster mushrooms, cleaned
1	red bell pepper, stemmed and seeded, cut into quarters lengthwise
1	green bell pepper, stemmed and seeded, cut into quarters lengthwise
1/4 cup	extra virgin olive oil
2 teaspoons	herbes de Provence or Italian herb blend
2 (15 oz.)	cans "recipe ready" diced tomatoes
1/2 teaspoon	each kosher salt and freshly ground pepper
1 pound	penne or other pasta
	freshly grated Parmesan or Asiago cheese for garnish

Insert the metal chopping blade in a Cuisinart® Food Processor. Place the parsley leaves in the work bowl and pulse about 10 times to chop. Remove the parsley and reserve. With the machine running, drop the garlic through the small feed tube and process 10 seconds to finely chop. Add the onion to the work bowl and pulse 8 to 10 times to chop. Remove the vegetables and reserve. Insert a medium (4-mm) slicing disc and using light pressure, slice the mushrooms, emptying the work bowl as needed. Set aside the mushrooms. Use light pressure to slice the red and green peppers and then place the pepper slices on a triple thickness of paper towels to drain.

In the Cuisinart® 12 1/2-inch Stir-Fry Pan, heat the olive oil over medium-high heat. Add the onions, garlic and mushrooms. Cook, stirring frequently, until the vegetables are tender and the liquid has evaporated, about 10 to 15 minutes. Add herbs and peppers and cook for 2 to 3 minutes. Add the tomatoes, salt and pepper. Reduce the heat to medium-low and cook, stirring occasionally, about 10 to15 minutes.

Bring 4 quarts of water with 2 teaspoons kosher salt to a boil in Cuisinart® Pasta Cooker. While the sauce simmers, cook the pasta al dente according to package instructions. Drain the pasta (reserving pasta cooking water) and add to the mushroom mixture in the stir-fry pan. Stir to combine and cook for 2 to 3 minutes, adding pasta cooking water (1/2 to 1 cup) as needed. Sprinkle with the reserved chopped parsley and serve with freshly grated cheese.

Nutritional information per serving:
Calories 352 (22% from fat)   carb. 61g   pro. 4g   fat 8g   sat. fat 1g   chol. 0mg   sod. 224mg   calc. 65mg   fiber 7g

BRAISED LAMB SHANKS WITH OLIVES 🍴🍴🍴

A "slow food" meal suitable for casual entertaining.

MAKES 4 GENEROUS SERVINGS

1/2 cup	Italian parsley leaves
2	onions (6 ounces each), peeled and quartered
3 (6 oz.)	carrots, peeled and cut to fit feed tube
4	lamb shanks (10 to 12 ounces each), trimmed of excess fat and fell (thin, membrane-like outer paper)
2 tablespoons	all-purpose flour
1 tablespoon	extra virgin olive oil
12 cloves	garlic, peeled and left whole
2 teaspoons	herbes de Provence
2 (15 oz.)	cans diced tomatoes, drained (reserve juice)
3/4 cup	dry white wine or vermouth
2 cups	fat free, less sodium chicken or beef stock
3/4 cup	drained pitted green olives
1/2 to 1 teaspoon	freshly ground pepper
	kosher salt to taste as needed

Preheat the oven to 325° F. Insert the metal chopping blade in the Cuisinart® Food Processor and place the parsley in the work bowl. Process 10 seconds to chop. Remove the parsley and reserve. Insert a medium (4-mm) slicing disc. Use medium pressure to slice the onions and carrots. Lightly dust the lamb shanks with the flour, shaking off any excess.

Over medium heat, heat the olive oil in a Cuisinart® 5 1/2-quart Sauté Pan or Casserole. Add the garlic cloves to the pan and cook until just lightly golden, about 4 to 5 minutes. Remove the garlic and reserve. Increase the heat to medium high and brown the lamb shanks well on all sides, letting the lamb brown for about 5 minutes on each side before turning. Remove the shanks and transfer to a platter. Drain off excess fat and discard. Reduce the heat to medium low and add the onions, carrots and herbes de Provence to the pan. Sauté until the vegetables are wilted and herbs are fragrant, 6 to 7 minutes. Add the diced tomatoes, wine, stock, reserved garlic and olives to the pan. Increase the heat and bring the sauce to a simmer. Return the lamb shanks to the pan, turning to coat with the sauce. Cover the pan and place in a preheated 325° F oven.

Bake the shanks for 2 1/2 hours, turning once or twice while baking. Stir in some of the reserved tomato juices as needed. Remove the cover and bake for an additional 45 minutes to reduce the sauce, turning the shanks once. Check the sauce and adjust the seasoning with freshly ground pepper and kosher salt as needed to taste. If serving at this time°, remove from the oven and allow to rest for 10 to 15 minutes. Spoon the skillet juices over the lamb shanks and sprinkle with the reserved chopped parsley to serve.

°*Braised Lamb Shanks with Olives may be prepared ahead and refrigerated. Remove and discard any accumulated hardened fat before reheating. Reheat the shanks and sauce in the covered skillet in the oven at 350° F until hot and bubbling, about 1 hour. Let the shanks rest and garnish as the recipe indicates to serve.*

Nutritional information per serving:
Calories 1101 (19% from fat) carb. 162g pro. 62g fat 24g sat. fat 5g chol. 132mg sod. 994mg calc. 391mg fiber 24g

Pecan Sesame Chicken

Crusty coated chicken without frying.

MAKES 4 SERVINGS

4	chicken breast halves, boneless, but with skin on
1 cup	pecans
2 slices	wheat bread, torn in pieces
1 large	egg
1 tablespoon	Dijon-style mustard
1/2 teaspoon	salt
1/4 teaspoon	black pepper

Preheat the Cuisinart® Toaster Oven to 375°F. Coat the drip pan lightly with cooking spray. You may lightly spray a 9 x 13 x 2-inch baking pan if you are using a traditional oven. Rinse and dry the chicken.

Place the pecans and bread in the work bowl of the Cuisinart® Food Processor fitted with the metal chopping blade. Pulse 5 times and then process 15 seconds until the mixture is fine crumbs. Remove the crumbs and place them a large plastic food storage bag.

Place the egg, mustard, salt and pepper in the work bowl and process until smooth, about 15 seconds. Transfer the mustard-egg wash to a pie plate.

Working with one chicken breast at a time, roll the chicken breast in the egg wash. Place the chicken piece in the bag with the crumb mixture and shake the bag to coat the chicken completely. Arrange the chicken breast on the prepared baking pan and repeat with the remaining chicken pieces.

Bake 35 to 40 minutes, until the chicken is golden brown and the juices run clear. Serve the chicken with the *Honey Mustard Sauce.*

Honey Mustard Sauce

MAKES ABOUT 1 CUP

1/2 cup	honey
1/4 cup	apple juice or cider
2 tablespoons	Dijon-style mustard
1 tablespoon	white balsamic vinegar

Place all of the ingredients in the work bowl of the Cuisinart ® Food Processor and process until emulsified.

Nutritional information per serving (1 piece chicken with 2 tablespoons sauce):
Calories 517 (41% from fat) carb. 22g pro. 53g fat 24g sat. fat 5g chol. 169mg sod. 365mg calc. 49mg fiber 1g

CATALAN ROASTED SEA BASS 🍴🍴🍴

Simply prepared fish with plenty of flavor.

MAKES 4 SERVINGS

	cooking spray (olive oil flavor)
4	sea bass fillets, 6 ounces each (you may use halibut, cod, or scrod)
1/4 cup	Italian parsley leaves, loosely packed
2 cloves	garlic, peeled
1 large	onion (8 ounces), peeled and halved
1 tablespoon	extra virgin olive oil
1/4 cup	dry white wine or vermouth
1 (15 oz.)	can diced tomatoes, drained
12	pitted Kalamata olives, halved
1/2 teaspoon	dried oregano
1/2 teaspoon	finely chopped orange zest
1/4 teaspoon	kosher salt
1/8 teaspoon	freshly ground black pepper

Preheat the Cuisinart® Toaster Oven to 450°F. Lightly coat a 10-inch gratin dish with cooking spray or olive oil. Arrange the sea bass in the dish in a single layer.

Insert the metal chopping blade in the Cuisinart® Food Processor. Place the parsley in the work bowl and pulse 10 times to chop. Remove the parsley from the work bowl and reserve. With the machine running, drop the garlic through the small feed tube and process 5 seconds to chop. Insert the medium (4-mm) slicing disc and slice the onion.

In a 12-inch Cuisinart® Skillet, heat the oil over medium high heat. Add the onion and garlic and sauté until light golden brown, about 5 minutes. Add the wine and simmer for 1 minute to reduce. Stir in the drained tomatoes, olives, oregano, zest, salt and pepper. Reduce the heat to low and simmer for 5 minutes. Spoon the sauce over the sea bass. Place in the preheated Cuisinart® Toaster Oven and bake for about 12 to 15 minutes, until the fish is opaque and flaky. Garnish with the reserved chopped parsley and serve immediately.

Nutritional information per serving:
Calories 290 (34% from fat) carb. 12g pro. 33g fat 11g sat. fat 2g chol. 71mg sod. 689mg calc. 67mg fiber 3g

BALSAMIC GLAZED PORK TENDERLOIN WITH PEPPERS

Tender medallions of pork are glazed with balsamic vinegar for this quick and easy entrée.

MAKES 4 SERVINGS

1/4 cup	Italian parsley leaves, washed and dried
2	red bell peppers, stemmed and cored, cut in quarters
2	yellow bell peppers, stemmed and cored, cut in quarters
1 pound	pork tenderloin, trimmed, cut into 8 equal pieces
1/4 cup	all-purpose flour
1 1/2 teaspoons	kosher salt, divided
1 teaspoon	freshly ground black pepper, divided
1 1/2 teaspoons	dried thyme, divided
1 tablespoon	unsalted butter
1 tablespoon	extra virgin olive oil
3/4 cup	fat free, less-sodium chicken broth or stock
3/4 cup	good quality aged balsamic vinegar

Insert the metal chopping blade in the Cuisinart® Food Processor. Place the parsley in the work bowl and pulse 10 times to chop. Remove the parsley and reserve. Insert a medium (4-mm) slicing disc into the food processor. Trim the bell pepper quarters to fit the feed tube as needed and arrange in the tube. Use light pressure to slice the peppers. Place the sliced peppers on a triple thickness of paper towels to dry.

Place the pork slices between 2 sheets of plastic wrap. Using a flat mallet/pounder, pound the pork slices to 1/4-inch thickness. (This can be done ahead, cover the meat tightly and refrigerate.) Combine the flour with 1 teaspoon of the salt, 1/2 teaspoon of the pepper and 3/4 teaspoon of the thyme. Just before cooking, lightly dredge the pounded pork slices in the flour mixture, shaking off any excess.

Heat the butter and oil in the Cuisinart® 12 1/2-inch Skillet until hot and bubbling. Place the pork slices in a single layer in the skillet and cook undisturbed for 2 1/2 minutes on each side, until nicely browned. Remove the pork to a platter and keep warm. Place the sliced peppers in the skillet with the remaining thyme, salt and pepper. Cook for 2 to 3 minutes over moderately high heat to soften and brown lightly. Remove the peppers and reserve. Add the stock and vinegar to the skillet and cook over high heat until reduced by half. Return the pork to the pan, turning to coat each side with the sauce, and top with the peppers. Cook just long enough to glaze and reheat the pork and peppers, about 1 to 2 minutes. Sprinkle with the reserved chopped parsley. Serve hot.

Nutritional information per serving:
Calories 288 (33% from fat) carb. 23g pro. 26g fat 11g sat. fat 4g chol. 74mg sod. 398mg calc. 40mg fiber 0g

BEEF FILLETS WITH GREEN PEPPERCORN SAUCE

A special occasion meal.

MAKES 6 SERVINGS

2 cloves	garlic, peeled
1	shallot peeled and quartered
1 teaspoon	kosher salt
1 teaspoon	freshly ground black pepper
6	beef tenderloin fillets, about 3/4-inch thick
2 tablespoons	olive oil
3/4 cup	beef stock or broth (low sodium)
1 cup	dry red wine, such as merlot
3 tablespoons	drained green peppercorns, rinsed and drained again
1/4 cup	cold unsalted butter, cut into 1/2-inch pieces

Place the garlic and shallot in the work bowl of the Cuisinart® Food Processor fitted with the metal chopping blade. Pulse to chop finely and reserve. Season the fillets on both sides with the salt and pepper.

Heat a 5 1/2-quart Cuisinart® Sauté Pan over medium high heat. When the pan is hot, add the oil and swirl to completely coat the pan. Add the fillets to the pan and brown on each side for about 2 to 3 minutes. Remove the fillets from the pan and cover.

To the pan add the stock, wine and chopped garlic and shallot. Cook over medium high heat for about 12 to 15 minutes. Return the fillets to the pan and cook 5 to 6 minutes on each side, until the fillets are done to taste. Remove the fillets to a warmed platter. With the pan off the heat, whisk in the green peppercorns, then gradually whisk in the cold butter, a few pieces at a time. Serve the Green Peppercorn Sauce over the fillets.

Nutritional information per serving:
Calories 482 (46% from fat)   carb. 2g   pro. 56g   fat 25g   sat. fat 10g   chol. 103mg   sod. 595mg   calc. 22mg   fiber 0g

MUSHROOM & PEPPER QUESADILLAS

Serve as an appetizer or as an entrée.
Serve with your favorite salsa, guacamole and sour cream garnish.

MAKES 6 QUESADILLAS

6 ounces	lowfat cheddar cheese
8 ounces	mushrooms, cleaned
1	green bell pepper, stemmed, seeded, cut in 4 slabs
1	red bell pepper, stemmed, seeded, cut in 4 slabs
1	yellow bell pepper, stemmed, seeded, cut in 4 slabs
1 clove	garlic, peeled
1 small	red onion, peeled, cut in quarters
2 tablespoons	vegetable or olive oil, divided
1 teaspoon	dried oregano
6 (9-inch)	flour tortillas (fat free)
1 1/2 cups	prepared fat free refried beans
	salsa, guacamole and sour cream for garnish

Insert the medium shredding disc in the Cuisinart® Food Processor. Use medium pressure to shred the cheese. Remove the cheese and reserve. Insert the slicing disc. Arrange the mushrooms in the large feed tube. Use light pressure to slice the mushrooms. Arrange the pepper slabs in the large feed tube. Use light pressure to slice the bell peppers. Remove the vegetables from the work bowl and reserve.

Insert the metal chopping blade in the food processor. With the machine running, drop the garlic through the small feed tube and chop 5 seconds. Add the onion and pulse 10 times until finely chopped.

Heat half the oil in a Cuisinart® 12-inch nonstick Skillet over medium high heat. Add the chopped garlic and onion and sauté until lightly browned, about 5 to 6 minutes. Add the remaining oil to the skillet and heat. Add the mushrooms and peppers to onion and garlic and sauté until the vegetables are tender, 4 to 6 minutes. Stir in the oregano. Spoon the vegetables into a bowl. Wipe out the skillet with a paper towel.

Heat one of the tortillas over medium heat in the skillet, about 30 seconds. Turn and sprinkle the tortilla with 1/4 cup of the reserved cheddar cheese. Top with 1/4 cup of the refried beans, and 1/6 of the sautéed vegetables. Fold the tortilla and cook until it is heated through. Repeat until all the tortillas and filling ingredients have been used. Serve with salsa, chopped avocado and sour cream for garnish.

Nutritional information per serving:
Calories 366 (31% from fat)   carb. 45g   pro. 19g   fat 13g   sat. fat 4g   chol. 18mg   sod. 839mg   calc. 341mg   fiber 7g

SHRIMP, CORN & BLACK BEAN QUESADILLAS

A winning combinations of flavors.

MAKES 8 QUESADILLAS – 24 PIECES

3/4 pound	cooked, shelled shrimp
1 1/2 cups (6 oz.)	lowfat cheddar cheese, shredded
1 cup	corn kernels (may use frozen, let thaw and pat dry)
1/2 cup	cooked and drained black beans
1/4 cup	chopped red onion
1/4 cup	chopped jalapeño pepper
1 teaspoon	dried oregano
8 (9-inch)	flour tortillas (fat free)
	olive oil for brushing tortillas (about 1/2-teaspoon per tortilla)
	salsa, guacamole and sour cream for garnish

Pat the shrimp dry to remove excess moisture and chop roughly. Place the shrimp in a medium bowl with the cheese, corn, black beans, red onion, jalapeño and oregano. Toss to combine. There should be about 4 cups of filling. Preheat the oven to 200° F and line a baking sheet with parchment or foil.

Lightly brush one side of each tortilla with olive oil. Spoon about 1/2 cup of shrimp filling evenly over half of each tortilla. Fold the tortillas in half and press gently.

Heat a Cuisinart® 10-inch nonstick Skillet over medium-high heat. Place a filled and folded quesadilla in the pan and cook for about 1 1/2 minutes on one side, until lightly browned and slightly crispy. The cheese will be slightly melted. Turn the quesadilla and cook for about 1 1/2 minutes on the second side. Transfer the cooked quesadilla to the prepared baking sheet and keep warm in the oven. Repeat until all the quesadillas are cooked. Use a sharp knife to cut each quesadilla into 3 equal portions, like pie slices. Serve warm with salsa, guacamole and sour cream as garnish.

Nutritional information per piece (24 pieces) – without garnish:
Calories 89 (20% from fat)   carb. 11g   pro. 7g   fat 2g   sat. fat 1g   chol. 30mg   sod. 207mg   calc 87mg   fiber 1g

MULTI-COLORED PASTA WITH SAGE & PROSCIUTTO RICOTTA FILLING FOR RAVIOLI

This is a beautiful dish for flavor and presentation.

MAKES ABOUT 3 POUNDS PASTA, 16 SERVINGS (4 OUNCE UNCOOKED)

6 to 7 cups	all-purpose flour, divided
3 large	eggs, divided
1 tablespoon	salt, divided
1/4 cup	water
1 (5 oz.)	beet, cooked, peeled and cut in 1-inch pieces
1/2 pound	fresh spinach leaves

Insert the metal chopping blade in the Cuisinart® Food Processor. Place 2 cups flour in the work bowl with 1 egg, 1 teaspoon of the salt, and 1/4 cup water. Process until the mixture forms a ball, about 30 seconds. If the dough is too dry to form a ball, add more water a tablespoon at a time. Remove the dough and wrap in plastic wrap. Place in the refrigerator for 30 minutes to allow the dough to rest.

Place the beet in the work bowl. Pulse to chop and then process until puréed. Repeat the pasta-making process with 2 more cups of the flour, another egg, and one teaspoon salt to make the beet pasta. Mix for about 90 seconds until the dough forms a ball. Remove the dough and wrap it in plastic wrap. Place in the refrigerator for 30 minutes.

Place about 2 ounces of the spinach in the work bowl and pulse to chop and then process until finely chopped, almost puréed. Keep adding the spinach to the work bowl, 2 ounces at a time and processing until all the spinach is chopped/puréed. Then repeat the pasta-making process with 2 cups of the remaining flour, the remaining egg and salt. Mix for 90 seconds, adding more flour 1 tablespoon at a time as necessary, if the dough is too moist. Wrap the dough in plastic wrap and refrigerate for 30 minutes.

Flatten each ball of dough slightly. With a pasta machine, use the flat roller setting to knead each ball of dough until smooth and flattened (using settings 1 and 2) to about 1/8-inch thick. Cut the rolled dough into 1/2-inch strips. Place the strips on a work surface, alternating each color strip and press together. Reroll the now stripped dough in the pasta machine until very thin.

To make ravioli:

Place the sheets of pasta on a lightly floured work surface. Place a mound (about 1 tablespoon) of *Sage & Prosciutto Ricotta Filling for Ravioli* or your favorite pasta filling every 2 inches. Cover with a second sheet of pasta dough and press gently to form ravioli. Cut into squares and press all sides with a fork to secure the filling inside the dough.

Boil the pasta gently to cook and serve with your favorite sauce.

Sage & Proscuitto Ricotta Filling page 104

Nutritional information per serving:
Calories 219 (6% from fat)   carb. 43g   pro. 7g   fat 2g   sat. fat 0g   chol. 40mg   sod. 288mg   calc. 23mg   fiber 2g

SAGE & PROSCIUTTO RICOTTA FILLING FOR RAVIOLI

MAKES 2 1/2 CUPS

2 cups	whole milk ricotta cheese, drained if there is visible whey
1/2 cup	freshly grated Asiago cheese
2 ounces	finely chopped prosciutto
1 large	egg, lightly beaten
2 tablespoons	chopped fresh parsley
15 to 20	fresh sage leaves, finely chopped
1 clove	garlic minced
1/2 teaspoon	kosher salt
1/4 teaspoon	freshly ground pepper

To finely chop the proscuitto, roll and then thinly slice into ribbons. Chop the ribbons finely. Place the ricotta, Asiago, prosciutto, egg, parsley, sage, garlic, salt and pepper in a medium bowl. Stir and mix until completely blended. Chill until ready to fill the ravioli.

Nutritional information per serving (1 tablespoon):
Calories 31 (65% from fat) carb. 1g pro. 2g fat 2g sat. fat 1g chol. 14mg sod. 68mg calc. 38mg fiber 0g

VEAL STIFADO

*Cook this Greek stew in your Cuisinart® Slow Cooker and serve along
with a green salad and crusty bread for a cold weather meal.*

MAKES ABOUT 10 CUPS

1/2 cup	all-purpose flour
1 teaspoon	kosher salt
1/2 teaspoon	freshly ground pepper
3 1/2 pounds	veal cubes (1 to 1 1/2-inch), trimmed of visible fat
3 tablespoons	extra virgin olive oil, divided
3 cloves	garlic, peeled and minced
1 pound	frozen small whole onions, thawed (or fresh, peeled)
1/4 cup	dry white vermouth or dry white wine (not chardonnay)
2 (15 oz.)	cans diced tomatoes in thick juices
1 whole	cinnamon stick (3-4 inches)
1 1/2 teaspoons	dried oregano
1 1/2 teaspoons	dried rosemary
1 1/2 teaspoons	dried thyme
1 teaspoon	ground cumin
1	bay leaf
1/4 cup	red wine vinegar
	feta cheese and freshly chopped parsley for garnish

Combine the flour, salt and pepper in a large bowl. Toss the veal cubes in the seasoned flour to coat lightly. Shake off and discard excess flour.

Heat 1 tablespoon of the oil in a Cuisinart® 12-inch Skillet over medium high heat. Working with one third of the veal at a time, brown the meat well on all sides, for about 4 to 5 minutes. As the cubes are browned, transfer the veal to the crock insert of the Cuisinart® Slow Cooker™. Repeat this process 2 more times using the oil as needed. In the same skillet, sauté the garlic and onions for 2 to 3 minutes, stirring in the wine and scraping up all the flavorful browned bits from the bottom of the pan. Add the sautéed onions, garlic and the liquid to the veal in the crock.

Stir in the tomatoes with their juices, cinnamon stick, oregano, rosemary, thyme, cumin, bay leaf and vinegar into the crock. Cover and cook on Low for 5 hours using the Timer Function — the Cuisinart™ Slow Cooker will automatically switch to *Keep Warm* to hold the stew until you are ready to serve.

Serve garnished with crumbled feta cheese and freshly chopped parsley.

Nutritional information per serving:
Calories 234 (32% from fat)   carb. 14g   pro. 25g   fat 8g   sat fat 2g   chol. 85mg   sod. 360mg   calc. 65mg   fiber 3g

GNOCCHI DI SPINACI RUSTICO
WITH GOLDEN POMODORO SAUCE

A light spinach and cheese dumpling made with breadcrumbs instead of flour.
If desired, add some freshly grated lemon zest to the dough.

MAKES ABOUT 60 DUMPLINGS, ABOUT 1/2-OUNCE EACH – 6 SERVINGS

5 ounces	Italian white bread (with crusts), in 1-inch cubes
6 ounces	Reggiano Parmesan cheese, cut in 1-inch pieces
1 teaspoon	freshly ground white pepper
1/2 teaspoon	freshly grated nutmeg
2 (10 oz.)	packages frozen chopped spinach, thawed

Place the bread in the work bowl of the Cuisinart® Food Processor fitted with the metal blade. Pulse to chop, then process until the bread becomes fine crumbs, about 1 minute. Transfer the bread crumbs to a bowl and reserve. With the machine running drop the cheese through the small feed tube and process 30 seconds until the cheese is very finely chopped. Add the cheese to the bread crumbs. Stir in the ground pepper and nutmeg and reserve.

Place the thawed spinach in a clean dark-colored kitchen towel (the spinach will leave stains). Squeeze all of the excess water out of the spinach. Place the well-squeezed spinach in the work bowl and pulse-chop until finely blended. Add the reserved bread crumbs and process 40 to 50 seconds to combine. (This may be done in 2 batches if you have a 7-cup or smaller food processor). Transfer the dough to a bowl and refrigerate 20 minutes.

Measure spinach dough into walnut-sized pieces. Lightly coat your hands with flour and shape the dough into rounds about 1/2-inch thick. Repeat until all the dough has been used. Place the rounds on a baking sheet lined with plastic wrap and refrigerate until ready to cook.

Bring lightly salted water to a boil in a Cuisinart® 6-quart Sauce Pot. Reduce the heat so that the boil is not rapid and add the dumplings. They will be cooked through when they float on the surface and are light. Serve the dumplings with *Golden Pomodoro Sauce* and freshly grated Reggiano Parmesan to pass.

Nutritional information per serving:
Calories 196 (37% from fat)   carb. 17g   pro. 14g   fat 8g   sat fat 5g   chol. 20mg   sod. 553mg   calc. 462 mg   fiber 3g

GOLDEN POMODORO SAUCE

MAKES ABOUT 4 CUPS

2 cloves	garlic, peeled
2 tablespoons	extra virgin olive oil
2 pounds	yellow tomatoes, cored, cut into 1-inch pieces
12 leaves	fresh basil
1 teaspoon	kosher salt
1/2 teaspoon	red pepper flakes
	freshly grated Parmesan cheese to taste

Insert the metal chopping blade in the Cuisinart® Food Processor. With the machine running, drop the garlic through the small feed tube and process 10 seconds to chop. Heat the olive oil in a Cuisinart® 5 1/2-quart Sauté Pan over medium low heat. Add the garlic and brown lightly, about 2 minutes. Add the tomatoes and cook until very soft, about 6 to 8 minutes.

Transfer the cooked tomatoes, basil leaves, salt and pepper flakes to the Cuisinart® Food Processor fitted with the metal blade. Pulse 15 to 20 pulses to chop. (If using a 7-cup or smaller processor you may do this in two batches.) Return the tomato mixture to the sauté pan and cook over low heat for about 5 minutes. Serve with *Gnocchi di Spinaci di Rustico.*

Nutritional information per serving:
Calories 55 (56% from fat) carb. 6g pro. 1g fat 4g sat fat 1g chol. 0mg sod. 177mg calc. 8mg fiber 1g

MEDITERRANEAN BRISKET OF BEEF 🍴🍴🍴

This full-flavored meat will melt in your mouth.

MAKES 8 TO 12 SERVINGS

3 cloves	garlic, peeled
2 pounds	onions, peeled, cut in half lengthwise
1	beef brisket, about 4 pounds
1 teaspoon	kosher salt
1 teaspoon	freshly ground pepper
1 tablespoon	extra virgin olive oil
12 ounces	white button or cremini mushrooms, cleaned and halved
1 teaspoon	dried thyme
1 teaspoon	dried basil
2 (15 oz.)	cans recipe ready diced tomatoes, drained (discard liquid)
1 cup	beef broth or stock (low-sodium, fat free)
1 pound	peeled baby carrots

Place the garlic in the work bowl of the Cuisinart® Food Processor fitted with the metal chopping blade and process 5 seconds to chop. Insert the thick (8-mm) slicing disc and slice the onions. Set aside the vegetables and reserve.

Use a sharp knife to score the "fat cap" of the meat so that it will not curl when browned. (Do not remove the fat, it helps to keep the meat moist and tender.) Season the meat on both sides with the kosher salt and pepper. Heat the olive oil in a Cuisinart® 12-inch Skillet over medium high heat. Brown the seasoned brisket for 5 to 6 minutes on each side. Remove the brisket and place it on a plate. Pour off the excess fat from the pan and discard. Place the pan over medium heat and add the onion/garlic mixture, the mushrooms, thyme and basil. Cook, stirring up all the good, flavorful browned bits in the pan, until the vegetables soften, about 6 to 8 minutes. Stir in the drained tomatoes and stock and cook for 4 to 5 minutes.

Place half the cooked vegetable mixture in the Cuisinart™ Slow Cooker ceramic pot. Place the browned brisket on top of the vegetables. Top with the carrots and the remaining cooked vegetable mixture including the liquid. Using the Timer Function, set the Cuisinart™ Slow Cooker to Low for 7 hours — the Slow Cooker will automatically switch to *Keep Warm* to hold the brisket and vegetables until ready to serve. Or, the brisket may be cooked on High using the Timer Function for 4 hours – it will automatically switch to *Keep Warm* to hold until ready to serve.

To serve, remove the brisket from the liquid and let it rest on a platter or cutting board loosely covered with foil. Strain the fat from the pan juices. This sauce can be served as is, or it can be thickened by reducing over heat. To thicken the sauce, strain it, reserving the vegetables, and transfer the liquid into a saucepan. Bring the sauce to a simmer and cook until it is reduced and thickened slightly. After the brisket has rested for about 10 minutes, slice thinly and serve with the sauce and vegetables.

Nutritional information per serving (based on 12 servings):
Calories 355 (21% from fat) carb. 16g pro. 54g fat 8g sat fat 2g chol. 98mg sod. 482mg calc. 56mg fiber 4g

CHICKEN & MUSHROOMS MADEIRA

An excellent entrée for that special occasion.

MAKES 6 SERVINGS

6	boneless, skinless chicken breast halves
1/2 cup	all-purpose flour
1 teaspoon	kosher salt
1/2 teaspoon	freshly ground black pepper
1/2 teaspoon	paprika
3 tablespoons	unsalted butter, divided
3 tablespoons	extra virgin oil, divided
2	shallots, peeled and chopped
2 cloves	garlic, peeled and chopped
2 cups	sliced mushrooms
3/4 cup	Madeira®
3/4 cup	chicken stock
1/4 cup	heavy cream
1/2 teaspoon	kosher salt
1/4 teaspoon	freshly ground pepper
1/2 cup	chopped fresh chives

Trim the chicken of all visible fat. Place individual pieces between 2 sheets of plastic wrap and pound to an even thickness with a flat pounder. Combine the flour with 1 teaspoon salt, 1/2 teaspoon pepper and paprika. Dredge the chicken in flour shaking off the excess and set aside.

Preheat the Cuisinart® Electric Skillet to 325°F and add half of the butter and oil to the skillet. When it is hot and bubbly, add the chicken and cook until browned, about 3 to 4 minutes on each side. Remove the chicken pieces and place on a warm platter. Cover loosely with foil and reserve.

Add the remaining butter and oil to the skillet. When hot, add the shallots and garlic and stir and cook for 2 minutes. Add the mushrooms and increase the heat to 375°F. Cook until the mushrooms are browned, about 3 to 5 minutes. Stir in the Madeira®, chicken stock and cream. Bring to a boil, reduce the heat to simmer and reduce the liquid by about half. Return the reserved chicken and any accumulated juices to the skillet, turning to coat the chicken. Season with salt and pepper and simmer for about 5 minutes. Sprinkle the chicken and sauce with chopped chives before serving.

Nutritional information per serving:
Calories 327 (48% from fat)   carb. 5g   pro. 38g   fat 18g   sat fat 7g   chol. 124mg   sod. 689mg   calc. 37mg   fiber 1g

BROCCOLI RABE OMELETTE

An elegant entrée for a light supper.

MAKES 4 TO 6 SERVINGS

1 (2 pounds)	bunch broccoli rabe
2 tablespoons	extra virgin olive oil
1 large clove	garlic, crushed
12 large	eggs
1/2 teaspoon	sea salt (or kosher salt)
1/4 teaspoon	freshly ground pepper
2 tablespoons	unsalted butter
	freshly grated Reggiano Parmesan or Grana Padano® cheese to taste

Trim the tough bottoms from the stems of the broccoli rabe. In a Cuisinart® 12-inch Skillet, heat the olive oil over low heat. Add the garlic and cook to brown, about 1 minute. Add the broccoli rabe, toss to coat in the oil, and cover and cook until tender, about 3 to 4 minutes. Stir occasionally. Remove the rabe from the pan and chop.

Whisk the eggs, salt and pepper in a large bowl to blend well. Melt the butter in the same skillet over medium low heat. Add the broccoli rabe to the skillet and spread evenly over the bottom. Pour the egg mixture over the broccoli rabe. Cook about 4 to 5 minutes until the eggs are softly set, tilting the skillet, and gently running a heatproof rubber spatula around the edges to allow the uncooked egg portion to flow underneath. Tilt the skillet and slide the omelet out onto a large warm platter, folding the omelette in half. Cut the omelette into wedges and serve. Garnish with freshly grated Reggiano Parmesan or Grana Padano® cheese.

For filled omelettes, cook the eggs, without the broccoli rabe, as directed above. When the eggs are nearly set, add the broccoli rabe and sprinkle with the cheese. Cook until the eggs are firmly set. Tilt the skillet and slide the omelette out onto a warmed platter, folding the omelette in half. Garnish with more cooked broccoli rabe and sprinkle with cheese.

Nutritional information per serving (based on 6 servings without cheese):
Calories 223 (53% from fat)   carb. 7g   pro. 18g   fat 12g   sat. fat 3g   chol. 425mg   sod. 317mg   calc. 317mg   fiber 4g

CREAMY PARMESAN RISOTTO

Enjoy this versatile creamy risotto!

MAKES 3 CUPS (SERVES 6 AS A SIDE DISH, 4 AS A FIRST COURSE, 2 AS AN ENTRÉE)

1 teaspoon	unsalted butter
1 teaspoon	extra virgin olive oil
1/3 cup	onion or shallot, finely chopped
1 cup	Arborio rice
1/3 cup	dry white wine or vermouth
3 cups	water, chicken or vegetable stock (you may use a combination if desired)
1/4 cup	heavy cream
1/4 cup	freshly grated Parmesan cheese
1/4 teaspoon	ground white pepper
1/4 cup	fresh chives or Italian parsley, chopped

Place the butter and olive oil in the rice cooking bowl of the Cuisinart™ Rice Cooker. Cover, turn on the cooker and wait one minute. Stir in the chopped onion and cover; cook 1 minute. Add the rice and stir to coat completely. Cover and cook 2 minutes. Stir in the wine and cover. Cook 2 to 3 minutes, until the wine is completely absorbed. Add the water or stock and stir. Cover and cook for 25 minutes, stirring 2 or 3 times during cooking. Cook until the rice cooker switches to *Keep Warm*. Stir in the heavy cream, Parmesan, and white pepper. Let stand on *Keep Warm* for 5 to 10 minutes. Sprinkle with the chopped fresh herbs and serve hot.

Nutritional information per side dish serving:
Calories 106 (38% from fat)   carb. 10g   pro. 4g   fat 4g   sat fat 2g   chol. 11mg   sod. 332mg   calc. 64mg   fiber 0g

MAPLE BALSAMIC GRILLED VEAL CHOPS

This entrée is quick and easy but filled with a depth of flavors.

MAKES 6 SERVINGS

1/4 cup	real maple syrup (not pancake syrup)
2 tablespoons	balsamic vinegar
2 tablespoons	olive oil
2 tablespoons	shallot, very finely minced
1 tablespoon	herbes de Provence
1/2 teaspoon	kosher salt
1/4 teaspoon	freshly ground pepper
6	loin or rib veal chops, each about 1-inch thick (about 8-10 ounces each)

Place the maple syrup, balsamic vinegar, oil, minced shallot, herbes de Provence, salt and pepper in a small bowl and whisk until emulsified.

Trim any excess fat from the veal using a sharp knife with a thin blade. Place the veal chops in the maple balsamic marinade, and turn to coat. Marinate for 20 to 30 minutes.

While the veal chops marinate, preheat the Cuisinart™ Grill/Griddle to *High/Sear*. When the grill is hot, arrange the veal chops evenly spaced on the grill. Grill for 6 to 8 minutes per side for medium rare. Remove the chops from the grill and let rest for a few moments before serving.

Nutritional information per serving (one chop):
Calories 461 (37% from fat)   carb. 11g   pro. 59g   fat 18g   sat. fat 6g   chol. 240g   sod. 327mg   calc. 29mg   fiber 0g

MEDITERRANEAN MUSSELS WITH LINGUINE ♙♙♙

Serving suggestion: serve with green salad, crusty bread and flavorful olive oil for dipping

MAKES 4 SERVINGS

2 pounds	fresh mussels in shells
1/4 cup	cornmeal
3/4 pound	linguine
1/2 cup	dry white vermouth or other dry white wine (not Chardonnay)
1/2 cup	clam broth
4 teaspoons	extra virgin olive oil
2	shallots, peeled and chopped
3 cloves	garlic, peeled and chopped
1 teaspoon	dried basil
1 teaspoon	dried oregano
1 (15.5 oz.)	can recipe ready diced tomatoes with juices
1/2 teaspoon	kosher salt
1/4 teaspoon	freshly ground black pepper
1/4 cup	freshly chopped Italian parsley
	lemon wedges for garnish

Rinse the mussels and discard any that are open or cracked. Scrub each with a stiff-bristled brush and place them in a medium bowl with the cornmeal. Add enough cold water to cover the mussels by 1-inch and stir gently. Let the mussels sit in the water with the cornmeal for 30 minutes. Drain and rinse. Remove the beards (pull off with your fingers or pliers/tweezers) and any visible debris from the shells. Discard soaking liquid.

Cook the pasta according to the package directions. Drain the pasta and reserve 1/2 cup of the pasta cooking water. Keep the pasta warm.

Combine the vermouth (or wine) and clam broth in the Cuisinart® 5 1/2-quart Sauté Pan and bring to a boil over high heat. Add the drained, cleaned mussels. Cover the skillet with a sheet of parchment or waxed paper and cook until the mussels are open, about 1 1/2 to 2 minutes. Check the mussels about every 30 seconds and transfer them to a bowl as they open up. Do not overcook the mussels. Cover loosely with the parchment or waxed paper and set aside. Over high heat, reduce the cooking liquid by two thirds. Pour the liquid through a strainer lined with a coffee filter to remove any sand or grit. Reserve the strained cooking liquid and wipe any grit from the pan with a paper towel.

Heat the olive oil in the same pan over medium heat. Add the chopped shallots, garlic, basil and oregano. Cook for 2 to 3 minutes, until the vegetables are softened and the herbs are aromatic. Stir in the tomatoes with their juices, the reserved mussel cooking liquid, salt and pepper. Bring this to a simmer and cook for 5 to 6 minutes, until somewhat thickened. Stir the reserved mussels and any accumulated juices and pasta into the sauce. Toss gently to coat completely and cook just to heat through, 2 to 3 minutes. If the sauce seems too thick, add a little of the reserved pasta cooking liquid.

Sprinkle with chopped parsley and garnish with lemon wedges. Serve hot.

Nutritional information per serving:
Calories 412 (16% from fat)   carb. 54g   pro. 28g   fat 7g   sat. fat 1g   chol. 42mg   sod. 770mg   calc. 81mg   fiber 3g

SEAFOOD & SAUSAGE PAELLA 🥄🥄🥄🥄

This is a beautiful entrée that your guests will savor and enjoy!

16	shrimp (18 to 20 count), peeled and deveined
12	sea scallops
12	steamer clams
12	mussels
1	halibut steak, about 1/2 pound
1 (15 oz.)	can artichoke hearts, drained on paper towels
1 teaspoon	saffron threads, crumbled
2 cups	fat free, low sodium chicken stock, heated
2 tablespoons	extra virgin olive oil, divided
12 ounces	low fat chicken chorizo or traditional chorizo, sliced 1/2-inch thick
1/2 cup	dry white vermouth or other dry white wine (not chardonnay)
2 cups	chopped onion
1 tablespoon	garlic, finely chopped
1 cup	red or green bell pepper, chopped
2 1/4 cups	basmati or other long grain white rice
2 cups	clam juice, heated
1 cup	water
2 to 3 tablespoons	fresh cilantro or parsley, chopped

Use a sharp knife to cut the shrimp partially through along the back, place in a bowl and set aside. Remove the tough muscle from the side of the scallops if necessary and slice the scallops in half horizontally. Set aside. Scrub the clams and mussels under cold water and debeard the mussels as necessary. Reserve. Skin and bone the halibut steak, cut into 1/2-inch thick slices and reserve. Cut the well-drained artichoke hearts in half or quarters and reserve.

Crumble the saffron threads and stir them into the hot chicken stock. Let this stand. Heat 1 tablespoon of the olive oil over medium high heat in the Cuisinart® 5 1/2-quart Casserole. When the oil is hot and shimmering, add the sliced chorizo. Cook the sausage until evenly browned, 4 to 5 minutes. Discard any excess fat that has been rendered. Add the vermouth, stirring to loosen the brown bits from the bottom of the casserole. Cook until the vermouth has reduced by half, 2 to 3 minutes. Remove the vermouth and sausage and reserve. Reduce the heat to medium low and add the remaining olive oil to the pan. When the oil is hot, add the chopped onions, garlic and red peppers to the pan and stir to coat with oil. Cover loosely and cook until the vegetables are softened, but not browned, about 5 to 8 minutes.

Stir in the rice and cook about 5 minutes, stirring frequently, until the rice is opaque. Return the sausage/wine mixture to the pan and stir in the chicken stock, clam juice and water. Cover and cook for 5 minutes. Stir in the reserved shrimp, scallops and halibut along with the artichokes and peas. Cover and cook 5 minutes longer. Uncover and arrange the clams and mussels, hinge side down, in the rice mixture. Cover and cook until the clams and mussels are open, the rice is tender and the seafood is cooked, about 7 to 10 minutes longer. Discard any unopened clams or mussels. Sprinkle with chopped cilantro.

Spoon the paella onto warmed plates and serve. The paella may be garnished with lemon and tomato wedges.

Nutritional information per serving:
Calories 526 (17% from fat) carb. 56g pro. 48g fat 10g sat. fat 2g chol. 157mg sod. 956mg calc. 117mg fiber 2g

ELEGANT BUT EASY BAKED SALMON

Quick and easy to prepare, but good enough for a special occasion.

MAKES 4 SERVINGS

	cooking spray
4 (6 oz.)	salmon fillets (choose fillets of similar thickness)
1 teaspoon	dried thyme
1/2 teaspoon	kosher salt
1/4 teaspoon	freshly ground pepper
4 ounces	crusty French bread, cut into 1-inch pieces
3 tablespoons	raspberry vinegar
2 tablespoons	Dijon-style mustard
1 tablespoon	granulated sugar
1 1/2 teaspoons	dry mustard
4 tablespoons	extra virgin olive oil

Preheat the oven to 400°F. Lightly coat a 13 x 9 x 2-inch baking dish with cooking spray. Arrange the salmon in the prepared dish, skin side down. Season with dried thyme, salt and pepper. Reserve.

Insert the metal blade in the Cuisinart® Food Processor. Place the bread in the work bowl. Process about 30 seconds until it is fine crumbs. Remove the crumbs from the work bowl and reserve. Place the vinegar, mustard, sugar and dry mustard in the work bowl and process 5 seconds to blend. With the machine running, add the oil through the feed tube and process 20 seconds to emulsify. Spread 1 tablespoon of the mustard sauce over each fillet, covering it completely. Press the breadcrumbs onto the fish.

Bake the salmon until it is cooked through and the crumb topping is browned and crispy, about 10 to 12 minutes. Transfer the salmon to warmed plates and drizzle with the remaining mustard sauce to serve.

Nutritional information per serving:
Calories 502 (53% from fat)   carb. 19g   pro. 39g   fat 29g   sat. fat 5g   chol. 115mg   sod. 574mg   calc. 24mg   fiber 0g

Chapter Six

ENCHANTING DESSERTS

Served with hot coffee, spiced tea or a dessert wine, desserts are the perfect ending to your meal. Think about the many delectable taste sensations you will find in these desserts—smooth, tangy lemon in a *Lemon Tart*, icy and crisp pears in *Fresh Pear Sorbet* and dense, velvety chocolate in *Chocolate Panini*. Is it any wonder we all look forward to dessert?

For special occasions, try a classic *Italian Spumone*, *Multi-Colored Biscotti* and *Ciocconocciola Cookies* (just try to say it!). Each will richly reward your efforts. Perfect for a lunchbox or office treat, *Mocha Chocolate Chip Cookies* are packed with rich flavors and a gratifyingly chewy texture. The recipes you will find in this chapter are a delight!

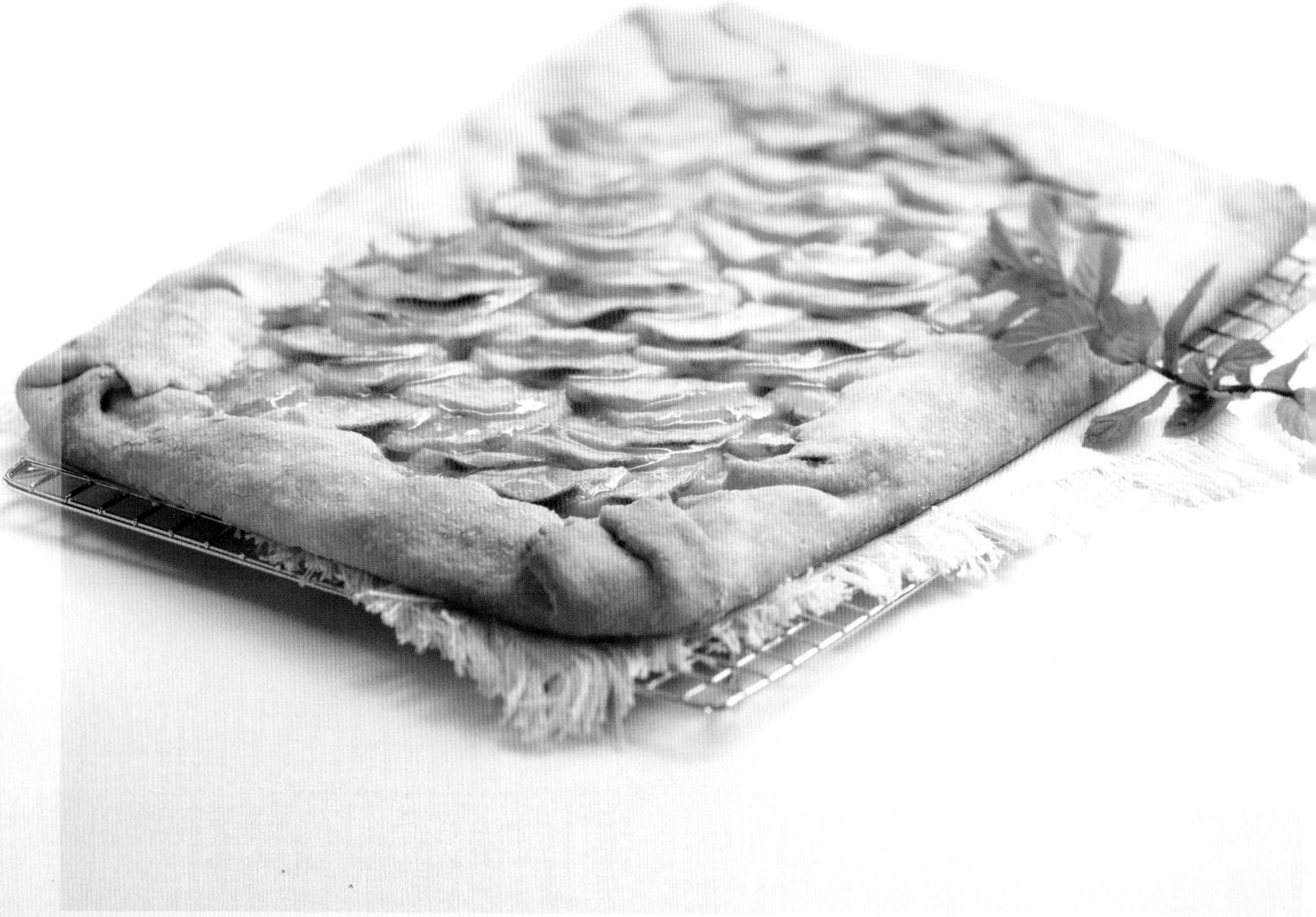

FRENCH APPLE PIE

Adapted from Master Chef Jacques Pépin's "La Technique" culinary encyclopedia (c.1989), this recipe for the famous French galette is a winner!

MAKES 8 SERVINGS (7 OZ. EACH)

Pastry:

2 cups	all-purpose flour
3/4 cup	cold unsalted butter
1/4 teaspoon	salt
1/2 teaspoon	sugar
1/3 cup	ice water

Fruit Filling:

5 large	apples or pears (you may use any baking apple or pear)
3 tablespoons	unsalted butter
1/3 cup	sugar
1/4 cup	apricot preserves
1 tablespoon	brandy

To make the pastry, place the flour, cold butter, salt and sugar in the Cuisinart® Food Processor work bowl fitted with the metal blade. Process 10 seconds until the mixture resembles coarse meal. With the motor running, pour the ice water through the feed tube in a steady stream and process 5 seconds just until the dough starts to form a ball. DO NOT OVERPROCESS.

Remove the dough to a sheet of wax paper, shape it into a disc and refrigerate, or use the dough immediately. Preheat the oven to 400°F. On a lightly floured work surface, roll out the dough to a 20 x 15-inch rectangle. Roll the dough onto a rolling pin to lift it off the surface and unroll it onto a lightly greased 12 x 16-inch baking sheet.

Insert the medium (4-mm) slicing disc into the food processor. Peel, halve and core the fruit. Stand the fruit halves in the feed tube and slice the fruit using medium pressure. Arrange the fruit slices overlapping in a single layer of diagonal rows. Leave about a 1 1/2-inch border of dough around the fruit. Fold the border onto the fruit. Dot the border with butter and sprinkle with sugar.

Bake until the crust is well-browned, about 70 minutes. Heat the apricot preserves and brandy over medium heat until the preserves have softened, about 3 minutes. Strain the brandy and preserve glaze through a sieve and brush it gently over the fruit. Serve warm.

Nutritional information per serving:
Calories 436 (45% from fat)   carb. 57g   pro. 4g   fat 22g   sat. fat 14g   chol. 58mg   sod. 81mg   calc. 18mg   fiber 3g

SPUMONE 🥄🥄🥄

A classic dessert made with layers of ice cream. This one is made with Cuisinart's no-cook ice cream recipes. If you want, you may add a fourth layer using strawberry ice cream and a larger loaf pan or ice cream mold.

MAKES 10 SERVINGS

2 cups	*Vanilla Ice Cream* (recipe follows)
1 cup	maraschino or glacéed cherries, drained, roughly chopped
2 1/2 cups	*Pistachio Ice Cream* (recipe follows)
2 1/2 cups	*Double Chocolate Ice Cream* (recipe follows)

Line an 8-cup (9 x 5 x 3-inch) loaf pan with a large sheet of plastic wrap, allow the excess to hang over the edges

Gently stir the cherries into the vanilla ice cream (or add the cherries during the last 2 minutes of mixing/freezing in the following recipe) and spread this in a layer in the lined pan. Top with a layer of pistachio ice cream and follow with a layer of chocolate ice cream. Cover completely with the plastic wrap and freeze until firm. Slice to serve.

Nutritional information per serving:
Calories 375 (63% from fat) carb. 32g pro. 4g fat 27g sat fat 15g chol. 85mg sod. 90mg calc. 104mg fiber 1g

VANILLA ICE CREAM

MAKES ABOUT 5 CUPS

1 cup	whole milk, well chilled
3/4 cup	granulated sugar
2 cups	heavy cream, well chilled
1 to 2 teaspoons	pure vanilla extract, to taste
1 tablespoon	rum, optional for *Spumone Ice Cream*

In a medium bowl, use a Cuisinart® Hand Mixer or a whisk to combine the milk and granulated sugar until the sugar is dissolved, about 1 to 2 minutes on low speed. Stir in the heavy cream and vanilla to taste. Add the rum if desired. Assemble the Cuisinart® Ice Cream Maker with a 1 1/2-quart capacity, and turn the machine on. Pour the vanilla mixture into the freezer bowl and mix/freeze until thickened, about 25 to 30 minutes. The ice cream will have a soft creamy texture. If desired, you may transfer the ice cream to an airtight container and place in the freezer for about 2 hours to "ripen" and firm.

Nutritional information per serving (1/2 cup):
Calories 237 (68% from fat) carb. 17g pro. 2g fat 18g sat. fat 11g chol. 69mg sod. 30mg calc. 60mg fiber 0g

PISTACHIO ICE CREAM

1 cup	whole milk, well chilled
3/4 cup	granulated sugar
2 cups	heavy cream, well chilled
1 teaspoon	pure vanilla extract
1/4 teaspoon	pure almond extract
1 cup	shelled pistachios, roughly chopped (may use plain or lightly salted)

In a medium bowl, use a Cuisinart® Hand Mixer on low speed, or a whisk to combine the milk and granulated sugar until the sugar is dissolved, about 1 to 2 minutes. Stir in the heavy cream, vanilla, and almond extract. Assemble Cuisinart® Ice Cream Maker with a 1 1/2-quart capacity, and turn the machine on. Pour the ice cream mixture into the freezer bowl and let it mix until thickened, about 25 to 30 minutes. During the last 5 minutes of freezing, add the pistachios. The ice cream will have a soft creamy texture. If desired, transfer the ice cream to an airtight container and place it in the freezer until firm, about 2 hours.

Nutritional information per serving (1/2 cup):
Calories 316 (70% from fat) carb. 21g pro. 4g fat 15g sat. fat 12g chol. 69mg sod. 130mg calc. 69mg fiber 1g

DOUBLE CHOCOLATE ICE CREAM

1 cup	whole milk
1/2 cup	granulated sugar
8 ounces	bittersweet or semi-sweet chocolate (your favorite), broken into 1/2-inch pieces
2 cups	heavy cream, well chilled
1 teaspoon	pure vanilla extract
2/3 cup	chopped white chocolate pieces (use white chocolate containing cocoa butter, not white confectionary coating)

Heat the whole milk until it is just bubbling around the edges (this may be done on the stovetop or in a microwave.) In a Cuisinart® Blender or Food Processor fitted with the metal chopping blade, pulse to process the sugar with the chocolate until the chocolate is very finely chopped. Add the hot milk and process until well blended and smooth. Transfer this to a medium bowl and let the chocolate mixture cool completely. Stir in the heavy cream and vanilla to taste. Chill for 30 minutes or longer.

Assemble the Cuisinart® Ice Cream Maker with a 1 1/2-quart capacity, and turn the machine on. Pour the chocolate mixture into the freezer bowl and let it mix until thickened, about 25 to 30 minutes. Add the white chocolate pieces during the last 5 minutes of freezing. The ice cream will have a soft creamy texture. If desired, transfer the ice cream to an airtight container and place it in the freezer until firm, about 2 hours.

Nutritional information per serving (1/2 cup):
Calories 387 (66% from fat) carb. 29g pro. 5g fat 30g sat. fat 18g chol. 95mg sod. 71mg calc. 161mg fiber 0g

LEMON TART

Fresh lemon flavor in a luxuriously simple tart.

MAKES ONE 11-INCH TART, 8 TO 12 SERVINGS

1 teaspoon	softened unsalted butter
1 1/2 cups	all-purpose flour
1/4 teaspoon	salt
1/2 cup	unsalted butter, cut into 1/2-inch pieces, frozen
1 large	egg yolk
5 tablespoons	ice water
5 medium	lemons
1 1/2 cups	granulated sugar
2 tablespoons	cornstarch
2 tablespoons	unsalted butter, at room temperature
5 large	eggs
1 teaspoon	pure vanilla extract

Butter an 11-inch springform tart pan with 1 teaspoon butter and set aside.

Insert the chopping metal blade in the Cuisinart® Food Processor. Place the flour and salt in the work bowl. Pulse 5 times. Add the butter and pulse 10 to 15 times until the butter and flour resembles a very coarse meal. Some bits of butter may be visible. Add the yolk and ice water and process until the mixture just begins to form a ball. Remove the dough and shape it into a disc. On a lightly floured surface, roll the dough into a circle, about 14-inches in diameter. Lift the dough carefully and place it in the prepared tart pan. Fold in the excess dough and press to form double thick sides.

Use a fork to evenly pierce the entire bottom of the dough. Freeze until the dough is firm, about 20 to 30 minutes.

Preheat the oven to 400°F. Line the chilled pastry with foil or parchment and fill with pie weights. Bake for 12 minutes. Remove the liner and weights and bake for an additional 5 minutes. Cool on a rack. Reduce the oven temperature to 350°F.

Remove the zest from the lemons with a vegetable peeler. Trim off any visible bitter white pith with a sharp knife. Juice the lemons and reserve (you will have about 3/4 cup lemon juice).

Insert the metal chopping blade in the Cuisinart® Food Processor. Place the lemon zest and 1/2 cup of the sugar in the work bowl and process until the zest is finely chopped, 1 to 2 minutes. Add the remaining sugar, cornstarch and butter. Process until smooth, about 30 seconds. Add the eggs, reserved lemon juice and vanilla. Process about 1 minute until well mixed. Place the baked tart shell (still in the pan) on a baking sheet lined with foil. Pour the lemon filling into the slightly cooled tart shell.

Bake in the preheated 350°F oven until golden brown and set, about 45 to 50 minutes. Allow the tart to cool on a wire rack at least 20 minutes before serving. Garnish with fresh lemon slices or berries and serve with slightly sweetened whipped cream if desired.

Nutritional Information per serving (based on 12 servings per tart):
Calories 294 (39% from fat) carb. 43g pro. 5g fat 13g sat. fat 7g chol. 134mg sod. 79mg calc. 43mg fiber 0g

MINI FRUIT CHEESECAKES 🍴🍴🍴

The perfect ending to a light lunch. Use raspberry, peach or blackberry jam for variety.

MAKES 6 SERVINGS

3 whole	graham crackers
1 tablespoon	unsalted butter
1 tablespoon	sugar
3 strips	lemon zest
1/4 cup	sugar
8 ounces	light cream cheese, cut into 1-inch pieces
2 teaspoons	fresh lemon juice
1/4 teaspoon	vanilla extract
1 large	egg
2 tablespoons	fruit jam of your choice

Preheat the oven to 325°F. Line 6 standard (1/2-cup) muffin pans with paper liners.

Break up the crackers and place them in a Cuisinart® Food Processor work bowl fitted with the metal blade. Process 30 seconds until the crackers are finely chopped. Add the butter and 1 tablespoon sugar and process 15 seconds until combined. Divide the cracker crust evenly among the prepared muffin cups and press it into the bottom of each cup. Bake 5 minutes. Remove from the oven and set aside.

Place the zest and 1/4 cup sugar into the food processor and process for 1 minute until finely chopped. Add the cream cheese, lemon juice and vanilla and process 30 seconds until smooth. Scrape the sides of the work bowl. With the motor running, add the egg through the feed tube and process 15 seconds to combine. Scrape the work bowl and process an additional 10 seconds.

Evenly pour the filling into the each muffin cup over the cracker crust and bake until set, about 20 minutes. Remove from the oven and cool the cheesecakes on a wire rack. Remove the cheesecakes from the muffin pans and refrigerate at least 4 hours. Before serving, stir the jam to make it spreadable and use 1 teaspoon to garnish each mini-cake.

Nutritional information per serving:
Calories 221 (42% from fat) carb. 27g pro. 6g fat 11g sat. fat 6g chol. 54mg sod. 307mg calc. 66mg fiber 1g

CIOCCONOCCIOLA COOKIES

A dense hazelnut and chocolate meringue cookie.

MAKES ABOUT 36 COOKIES

1 pound	blanched hazelnuts, toasted
1 pound	sifted powdered sugar
1/4 cup	unsweetened cocoa
3 large	egg whites
1/2 teaspoon	cream of tartar

Preheat the oven to 300°F. Line 2 baking sheets with parchment paper.

Place the nuts in a Cuisinart® Food Processor fitted with the metal blade. Pulse to chop and then process until the hazelnuts are finely ground. (If you have a 7-cup processor, you may do this in 2 or 3 batches.) Transfer the ground hazelnuts to a large bowl and stir in the sifted powdered sugar and unsweetened cocoa. Reserve.

Using a Cuisinart® Hand Mixer, whip the egg whites with the cream of tartar until they form stiff peaks, about 3 minutes. Fold in the reserved ground nut and sugar mixture. Drop the dough in walnut-sized balls (about 1 3/4 tablespoons) onto the prepared baking sheets.

Bake the cookies until firm and dry, about 45 minutes. Let the cookies stand 2 to 3 minutes, then place them on a wire rack to cool completely. Store the cookies in a tightly sealed container.

Tip: For a "fancier" cookie, melt semi-sweet or bitter-sweet chocolate and lightly drizzle the cooled cookies with just a little of the melted chocolate in random patterns.

Nutritional information per cookie:
Calories 136 (53% from fat) carb. 15g pro. 2g fat 9g sat. fat 1g chol. 0mg sod. 15mg calc. 25mg fiber 1g

MULTI-COLOR BISCOTTI (HOLIDAY BISCOTTI)

Easy to prepare and colorful for the holidays, delicious any time of the year. For a change, try these with dried blueberries and almonds, or dried tart cherries and hazelnuts.

MAKES ABOUT 2 DOZEN BISCOTTI

	cooking spray
1 1/2 cups	all-purpose flour
1/4 cup	cornstarch
1/2 teaspoon	baking powder
2 large	eggs
3/4 cup	sugar
1 tablespoon	vanilla extract
1 teaspoon	fresh lemon juice
1/8 teaspoon	salt
1/2 cup	shelled white pistachios
1/2 cup	dried cranberries

Preheat the oven to 350°F. Combine the flour, cornstarch and baking powder in a small bowl and reserve. Line two baking sheets with parchment paper, non-stick baking liners or spray with cooking spray.

Place the eggs, sugar, vanilla extract, lemon juice and salt in a large mixing bowl. Using the Cuisinart® Hand Mixer, start on low speed and gradually increase to medium speed, and beat until the batter is thick and smooth, about 2 minutes. Add the dry ingredients to the batter in 3 additions, mixing on low for 30 seconds after each addition. Add the pistachios and cranberries and continue on low speed until just blended.

Divide the dough in half. Place each half on the baking sheet and shape into 10 x 3-inch rectangles. Bake until a toothpick inserted in the center comes out clean, about 12 to 14 minutes. The tops of the rectangles should not be browned. Do not over bake or the biscotti will be too dry. Remove the biscotti from the oven and cool 10 minutes on the baking sheets.

Cut each rectangle into 12 equal slices. Place the cookies cut side down on the baking sheets. Bake for an additional 11 to 13 minutes, until crisp. Remove the biscotti from the baking sheets and cool on wire racks. When completely cool, store the biscotti in an airtight container.

Nutritional information per biscotti:
Calories 90 (20% from fat) carb. 16g pro. 2g fat 2g sat. fat 0g chol. 23mg sod. 24mg calc. 7mg fiber 1g

FRESH PEAR SORBET

Serve with chocolate sauce and fresh raspberries, or with our White Chocolate Chunk Ginger Snaps.

MAKES ABOUT 4 1/2 CUPS

1 1/2 cups	sugar
3/4 cup	water
1	vanilla bean, split lengthwise
2 strips	lemon zest (each about 1/2 x 3-inches), bitter white pith removed
2 1/4 pounds	ripe pears, peeled, cored and quartered
2 tablespoons	light corn syrup
1 tablespoon	fresh lemon juice

Place the sugar and water in a Cuisinart® 2 3/4-quart Saucepan and place over medium heat. Stir gently until the sugar dissolves. Add the vanilla bean, lemon zest and pears and cover and cook, stirring occasionally, until the pears are tender, about 10 minutes. Remove the vanilla bean (you may dry and place the bean in your sugar canister for vanilla sugar) and discard the zest. Reserving the poaching liquid, transfer the pears to a Cuisinart® Blender and process 1 minute until smooth. Combine the poaching liquid, pear purée, corn syrup and lemon juice in a bowl. Cover and chill until very cold, at least 1 hour.

Assemble a Cuisinart® Automatic Frozen Yogurt-Ice Cream and Sorbet Maker. Turn the machine on and add the chilled pear mix. Mix until the ice cream thickens, about 25 to 30 minutes. Turn the machine off and spoon the ice cream into an airtight container. Place this in the freezer until it is firm, about 2 hours. Allow the sorbet to sit at room temperature for 10 minutes before scooping to serve.

Nutritional information per serving:
Calories 216 (2% from fat)   carb. 56g   pro. 1g   fat 1g   sat. fat 0g   chol. 0mg   sod. 4mg   calc. 18mg   fiber 3g

WHITE CHOCOLATE CHUNK GINGER SNAPS

A wonderful addition to your holiday cookie assortment, crystallized ginger and white chocolate chunks add something special to an old favorite.

MAKES ABOUT 60 COOKIES

4 ounces	good quality white chocolate, broken into 1-inch pieces, chilled
3 ounces	candied ginger
4 cups	all-purpose flour
1/2 teaspoon	salt
2 1/4 teaspoons	baking soda
2 1/2 teaspoons	ground ginger
1 1/4 teaspoons	ground cinnamon
1 teaspoon	ground allspice
1/2 cup	unsalted butter, at room temperature
1/2 cup	vegetable shortening
2 1/2 cups	granulated sugar, divided
1/2 cup	molasses
2 large	eggs

Preheat the oven to 325°F. Line 2 large baking sheets with parchment paper. In a Cuisinart® Food Processor fitted with the metal chopping blade use quick pulses 10 to 15 times to coarsely chop the white chocolate. Remove the chocolate and reserve. Place the ginger in the work bowl and quickly pulse 15 to 20 times to chop the candied ginger into small bits. Remove the ginger and reserve. Add the flour, salt, baking soda and ground spices to the processor and process for 30 seconds to quick sift. Remove the dry ingredients and reserve.

With a Cuisinart® Hand Mixer, beat together the butter, shortening and 2 cups of the sugar in a 3-quart Cuisinart® Mixing Bowl, until the mixture is light and fluffy. Add the molasses and beat for 30 seconds. Beat in the eggs, one at a time, beating well after each addition. On a low speed, add the dry ingredients to the creamed ingredients in 4 separate additions, beating after each addition to combine. Add the white chocolate chunks and the candied ginger bits and beat until just blended.

Put the remaining 1/2-cup sugar in a small bowl. Form the dough into 1-ounce balls (about the size of a walnut) and roll in the sugar. Arrange the balls on the baking sheets about 3 inches apart and flatten slightly with the bottom of a glass. Bake the cookies in the middle of the oven for 10 to 12 minutes. The cookies will be puffed and golden and soft. Let the cookies cool on baking sheets for 5 minutes, then transfer them to a rack to cool. Store the cookies between sheets of waxed paper in an airtight container.

Nutritional information per cookie:
Calories 112 (32% from fat)   carb. 18g   pro. 1g   fat 4g   sat.fat 2g   chol. 12mg   sod. 67mg   calc. 20mg   fiber 0g

MOCHA CHOCOLATE CHIP COOKIES

This delicious "cookie jar" type cookie is certain to become a family favorite.

MAKES 3 1/2 DOZEN COOKIES

1 1/2 tablespoons	instant coffee granules or instant espresso powder
1 1/2 tablespoons	unsweetened cocoa powder
2 tablespoons	hot water
2 1/4 cups	all-purpose flour
1 1/4 teaspoons	baking soda
1/4 teaspoon	salt
1 cup	unsalted butter, cut in 8 pieces, at room temperature
3/4 cup	firmly packed light brown sugar
3/4 cup	sugar
2 large	eggs
1/2 teaspoon	pure vanilla extract
1 cup	pecan halves (may be toasted)
1 1/2 cups	semi-sweet chocolate morsels (you may use half white chocolate morsels if desired)

Preheat the oven to 350°F. Line 2 baking sheets with parchment paper.

Combine the instant coffee granules, cocoa and water in a small bowl and stir to blend. Reserve. Combine the flour, soda and salt in a small bowl, stir to blend and reserve.

Place the butter and sugars in the Cuisinart® Food Processor fitted with the metal chopping blade. Process about 1 minute until the mixture is smooth and creamy. Scrape the work bowl and process 30 seconds longer. Add the coffee, cocoa and water mix, eggs and vanilla. Process 30 seconds and scrape the sides of the work bowl. Process 20 seconds longer and scrape the work bowl again. Pour the dry ingredients over the top of the creamed ingredients. Top with the cooled pecans and chocolate chips. Pulse until the flour, nuts and chocolate chips are just blended — do not overprocess! If there is still a sprinkling of flour showing, stir this in with a spatula.

Drop the dough by rounded spoonfuls about the size of a walnut, 2 inches apart, on the prepared baking sheets. Bake until golden, about 16 to 18 minutes. Cool slightly on the baking sheet and then transfer to a wire rack to cool completely. Store the cookies in an airtight container.

Nutritional information per serving:
Calories 155 (50% from fat) carb. 18g pro. 1g fat 9g sat. fat 4g chol. 22mg sod. 52mg calc. 8mg fiber 2g

CHOCOLATE PANINI 🥄🥄

A quick and simple dessert that will bring rave reviews.

MAKES 2 PANINI SANDWICHES (SERVES 4)

4 slices	crusty country Italian loaf (each about 8 x 4 x 1/2-inch)
2 tablespoons	unsalted butter, melted
4 ounces	bittersweet or semisweet chocolate, chopped finely (1/8-inch pieces) If desired, you may use half bittersweet chocolate and half white chocolate.
	powdered sugar for dusting
	cinnamon for dusting

Preheat the Cuisinart™ Griddler™ in the closed griddle position to 350°F.

Brush one side of each slice of bread with the melted butter. Place 2 slices of bread on the work surface, buttered side down. Top each slice evenly with chopped chocolate. Place the 2 remaining bread slices on top of the chocolate, buttered side up.

Carefully place each panini on the bottom griddle plate of the Cuisinart™ Griddler™. Close the Griddler using medium pressure. Bake the panini for 5 minutes – until the chocolate is melted and the bread is toasted golden brown and crispy.

Remove the panini, cut each into quarters and dust lightly with powdered sugar and cinnamon. Serve hot, but not immediately as the melted chocolate can burn the tongue.

Nutritional information per serving:
Calories 285 (50% from fat)   carb. 32g   pro. 7g   fat 18g   sat fat 10g   chol. 16mg   sod. 211mg   calc. 25mg   fiber 1g

INDEX